About the Author

Born in Germany, Edgar Rothermich studied music and sound en[gineering] prestigious Tonmeister program at the Berlin Institute of Technology (TU) [and] University of Arts (UdK) in Berlin where he graduated in 1989 with a Master's Degree. He worked as a composer and music producer in Berlin, and moved to Los Angeles in 1991 where he continued his work on numerous projects in the music and film industry ("The Celestine Prophecy", "Outer Limits", "Babylon 5", "What the Bleep Do We Know", "Fuel", "Big Money Rustlas").

For the past 20 years Edgar has had a successful musical partnership with electronic music pioneer and founding Tangerine Dream member Christopher Franke. Recently in addition to his collaboration with Christopher, Edgar has been working with other artists, as well as on his own projects.

In 2010 he started to release his solo records in the "Why Not …" series with different styles and genres. The current releases are "Why Not Solo Piano", "Why Not Electronica", "Why Not Electronica Again", and "Why Not 90s Electronica". This previously unreleased album was produced in 1991/1992 by Christopher Franke. All albums are available on Amazon and iTunes, including the 2012 release, the re-recording of the Blade Runner Soundtrack.

In addition to composing music, Edgar Rothermich is writing technical manuals with a unique style, focusing on rich graphics and diagrams to explain concepts and functionality of software applications under his popular GEM series (Graphically Enhanced Manuals). His bestselling titles are available as printed books on Amazon, as Multi-Touch eBooks on the iBooks Store and as pdf downloads from his website.

(some manuals are also available in Deutsch, Español, 简体中文)

www.DingDingMusic.com   GEM@DingDingMusic.com

About the Editor

Many thanks to Tressa Janik for editing and proofreading this manual.

Special Thanks

Special thanks to my beautiful wife, Li, for her love, support, and understanding during those long hours of working on the books. And not to forget my son, Winston. Waiting for him during soccer practice or Chinese class always gives me extra time to work on a few chapters.

The manual is based on Logic Pro X v10.2.1
Manual: Print Version 2016-0131
ISBN-13: 978-1523485512
ISBN-10: 1523485515

About the GEM (Graphically Enhanced Manuals)

UNDERSTAND, not just LEARN

What are Graphically Enhanced Manuals? They're a new type of manual with a visual approach that helps you UNDERSTAND a program, not just LEARN it. No need to read through 500 pages of dry text explanations. Rich graphics and diagrams help you to get that "aha" effect and make it easy to comprehend difficult concepts. The Graphically Enhanced Manuals help you master a program much faster with a much deeper understanding of concepts, features, and workflows in a very intuitive way that is easy to understand.

All titles are available in three different formats:

.... pdf downloads from my website www.DingDingMusic.com/Manuals

.... multi-touch iBooks on Apple's iBooks Store

.... printed books on Amazon.com

(some manuals are also available in Deutsch, Español, 简体中文)

For a list of all the available titles and bundles: www.DingDingMusic.com/Manuals

To be notified about new releases and updates, subscribe to subscribe@DingDingMusic.com

About the Formatting

I use a specific color code in my books:

Green colored text indicates keyboard shortcuts or mouse actions. I use the following abbreviations: **sh** (shift key), **ctr** (control key), **opt** (option key), **cmd** (command key). A plus (+) between the keys means that you have to press all those keys at the same time.

sh+opt+K means: Hold the shift and the option key while pressing the K key.

(light green text in parenthesis indicates the name of the Key Command)

Brown colored text indicates Menu Commands with a greater sign (➤) indicating submenus.

Edit ➤ Source Media ➤ All means "Click on the Edit Menu, scroll down to Source Media, and select the submenu All.

Blue arrows indicate what happens if you click on an item or popup menu

Table of Contents

1 - Introduction

About This Book

Although the Logic Pro X 10.2.1 update doesn't have a high-profile addition like the Alchemy Plugin, it is still packed with tons of new features and improvements, besides the usual bug fixes. The Logic team did an outstanding job with adding all those new features and improvements that might seem just like minor tweaks, but they will definitely have a big impact on your workflow, no matter what type of music you are producing with Logic.

➡ Official Release Notes

For a comprehensive list of all the new stuff, you can access the official Release Notes directly from inside Logic by selecting the Main Menu **Help ➤ Release Notes**, which opens your web browser displaying the list on Apple's website.
https://support.apple.com/en-us/HT203718

➡ Why this Book?

So why did I write this book when all the new features and improvements are listed in the official Release Notes.

● Graphically Enhanced

The Release Notes only provide a short description of the new features or the changes. In this book, I provide a more in-depth explanation with lots of graphics, screenshots, and diagrams, and sometimes additional in-depth discussions of the topic to better understand the changes. You will have a "clear picture" of the changes right away and can start using it immediately.

● Hidden Features

The Release Notes often forget to list a few features, so whatever additional changes I stumbled over, found online, or what other users discovered on the various Logic forums, I will also list it here.

Free

I make the pdf and iBooks version of this book available for free - not only as a way to boost my Karma, but also to give back to the Logic community who supported me so far by purchasing my other Logic books.

 If you are new to my style of writing Graphically Enhanced Manuals and enjoy this book, then don't forget to check out those Logic books on my website
http://LogicProGem.com

If you've never read any of my other books and you aren't familiar with my Graphically Enhanced Manuals (GEM) series, let me explain my approach. As I mentioned at the beginning, my motto is:

"UNDERSTAND, not just LEARN"

Other manuals (original User Guides or third party books) often provide just a quick way to: "press here and then click there, then that will happen ... now click over there and something else will happen". This will go on for the next couple hundred pages and all you'll do is memorize lots of steps without understanding the reason for doing them in the first place. Even more problematic is that you are stuck when you try to perform a procedure and the promised outcome doesn't happen. You will have no understanding why it didn't happen and, most importantly, what to do in order to make it happen.

Don't get me wrong, I'll also explain all the necessary procedures, but beyond that, the understanding of the underlying concept so you'll know the reason why you have to click here or there. Teaching you "why" develops a much deeper understanding of the application that later enables you to react to "unexpected" situations based on your knowledge. In the end, you will master the application.

And how do I provide that understanding? The key element is the visual approach, presenting easy to understand diagrams that describe an underlying concept better than five pages of descriptions.

The Visual Approach

Here is a summary of the advantages of my Graphically Enhanced Manuals that set them apart from other books:

 **Better Learning**

 **Better Value**

☑ Graphics, Graphics, Graphics

Every feature and concept is explained with rich graphics and illustrations that are not found in any other book or User Guide. These are not just a few screenshots with arrows in it. I take the time to create unique diagrams to illustrate the concepts and workflows.

☑ Knowledge and Understanding

The purpose of my manuals is to provide the reader with the knowledge and understanding of an app that is much more valuable than just listing and explaining a set of features.

☑ Comprehensive

For any given feature, I list every available command so you can decide which one to use in your workflow. Some of the information is not even found in the app's User Guide.

☑ For Beginners and Advanced Users

The graphical approach makes my manuals easy to understand for beginners, but still, the wealth of information and details provide plenty of material, even for the most advanced user.

☑ Three formats

No other manual is available in all three formats: PDF (from my website), interactive multi-touch iBooks (on Apple's iBooks Store), and printed book (on Amazon).

☑ Interactive iBooks

No other manual is available in the enhanced iBooks format. I include an extensive glossary, also with additional graphics. Every term throughout the content of the iBook is linked to the glossary term that lets you popup a little window with the explanations without leaving the page you are currently reading. Every term lists all the entries in the book where it is used and links to other related terms.

☑ Up-to-date

No other manual stays up to date with the current version of the app. Due to the rapid update cycles of applications nowadays, most books by major publishers are already outdated by the time they are released. I constantly update my books to stay current with the latest version of an app.

☑ Free Updates (pdf, iBook only)

No other manual provides free updates, I do. Whenever I update a book, I email a free download link of the pdf file to current customers. iBooks customers will receive an automatic update notification, and 24 hours after a new update, the printed book will be available on Amazon. They are print-on-demand books, which means, whenever you order a book on Amazon, you get the most recent version and not an outdated one that was sitting in a publisher's warehouse.

Self-published

As a self-published author, I can release my books without any restrictions imposed by a publisher. Rich, full-color graphics and interactive books are usually too expensive to produce for such a limited audience. However, I have read mountains of manuals throughout the 35 years of my professional career as a musician, composer, sound engineer, and teacher, and I am developing these Graphically Enhanced Manuals (GEM) based on that experience, the way I think a manual should be written. This is, as you can imagine, very time consuming and requires a lot of dedication.

However, not having a big publisher also means not having a big advertising budget and the connections to get my books in the available channels of libraries, book stores, and schools. Instead, as a self-published author, I rely on reviews, blogs, referrals, and word of mouth to continue this series.

If you like my "Graphically Enhanced Manuals", you can help me promote these books by referring them to others and maybe taking a minute to write a review on Amazon or the iBooks Store.

Thanks, I appreciate it:

http://amzn.to/1sP8jvl   http://bit.ly/1oJ7ftQ

Disclaimer: As a non-native English speaker, I try my best to write my manuals with proper grammar and spelling. However, not having a major publisher also means that I don't have a big staff of editors and proofreaders at my disposal. So, if something slips through and it really bothers you, email me at <GrammarPolice@DingDingMusic.com> and I will fix it in the next update. Thanks!

LogicProGEM

Please check out my Logic site "**LogicProGEM**". The link "Blog" contains all the free Logic Articles that I have published on the web and continue to publish. These are in-depth tutorials that use the same concept of rich graphics to cover specific topics related to the use of Logic.

http://LogicProGEM.com

Bug Fixes

The Logic Pro X v10.2.1 update comes with a ton of bug fixes. Lots of them are listed in the official Release Notes, but I'm sure there are much more. Some of them are "high profile" bugs that users were eagerly waiting to get fixed. For example:

▶ Zoom Bug
▶ Go To Position Window Bug
▶ Issues with IR Files in Space Designer

In this book, I cover mainly the new features and changes and only mention a few bug fixes. If you want to find out if your "favorite" bug is fixed, just try it in LPX 10.2.1. If not, keep on reporting to the official feedback page at http://www.apple.com/feedback/logic-pro.html

Responsiveness

The Release Notes contain many items that refer to the various places in Logic that are much more responsive and faster. Here are just a few:

☑ Logic takes less time to analyze tracks with a large number of regions when Flex is enabled.
☑ More responsive when rubber-band selecting large numbers of notes in the Piano Roll
☑ More responsive when using the Pencil to draw in a series of notes in the Step Editor
☑ More responsive when zooming in projects that contain a large amount of automation
☑ More responsive when drag-copying or moving automation at high zoom levels
☑ More responsive when rearranging the order of tracks in the track header in projects that contain a large amount of automation
☑ More responsive when using a EuCon control surface with projects that contain a large number of tracks
☑ More responsive when horizontally dragging automation points in projects that contain a large amount of automation
☑ More responsive when scrolling in the Main window with a large number of tracks, regions, or automation
☑ More responsive when redoing a Comp selection after undoing it
☑ More responsive when renaming a channel strip while Logic is playing

Support for Standards

Support for WAVE RF 64

Logic now supports the extended audio file format WAVE RF 64.

Here are a few facts:
- ▶ WAVE RF64 (introduced in 2006) is an extension of the Microsoft WAVE format and its professional version BWF (Broadcast Wave Format).
- ▶ The term MBWF (Multichannel BWF) is also used instead of RF64.
- ▶ The audio format allows file sizes to exceed 4GB and allows for up to 18 audio channels.

Further reading:
- https://en.wikipedia.org/wiki/RF64
- https://tech.ebu.ch/docs/tech/tech3306-2009.pdf

Support for Audio Units 3

Audio Units

At last year's WWDC (World Wide Developer Conference), Apple showed the new AU3 standard and even demoed some features with a special Logic Pro X version. However, in this new LPX 10.2.1 update, I cannot find any mention of AU3 or any changes under the hood regarding that new standard. So we will see if more information comes out later or if some Logic users will find out more about it at some point.

Here is a link to the video on that presentation https://developer.apple.com/videos/wwdc/2015/?id=508

Besides all the in-depth coding information in the video, there are a few tidbits that sounded interesting, even for us non-coders:

- ☑ The new extension (AU3) is "almost completely compatible" with the existing one (AU2)
- ☑ AU3 runs as separate processes and won't crash Logic
- ☑ Support for 256 MIDI Cables with each having 16 MIDI Channels between AU and Host (send/receive MIDI on a Plugin?)
- ☑ At 4:30 is a short Logic demo with an "experimental version" of Logic
- ☑ AU Plugins are compatible between iOS and OSX
- ☑ The new AU3 Plugins can be purchased through the App Store

Support for Lua Script

Logic (and MainStage) now support Lua script files. As soon as a supported Device is connected, Logic detects it and automatically generates controller assignment.

This new support has something to do with the following note from the Logic Release Notes:

"You can now use Smart controls to automatically configure how Logic interacts with various MIDI controllers and keyboards".

650 New Apple Loops

Logic Pro X 10.2.1 includes over 650 new Apple Loops in a variety of dance and popular music genres. Those sounds aren't downloaded with the app. You have to install them separately:

Once you open the new Logic 10.2.1, go to the new Main Menu *Logic Pro X ➤ Sound Library ➤ Open Sound Library Manager...* ❶ to open the Sound Library Manager window ❷. In addition to any sounds that you haven't downloaded yet previously, you will see new genres in the Apple Loops category ❸.

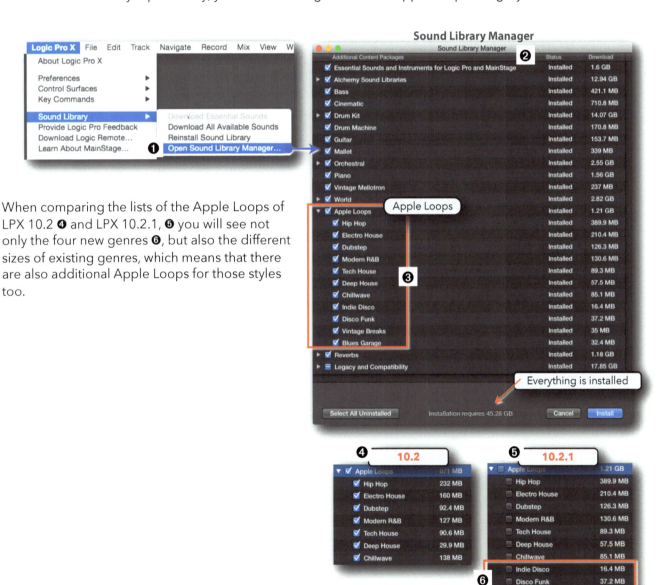

When comparing the lists of the Apple Loops of LPX 10.2 ❹ and LPX 10.2.1, ❺ you will see not only the four new genres ❻, but also the different sizes of existing genres, which means that there are also additional Apple Loops for those styles too.

If you don't have enough space on your boot drive to install all the content, or like to have it on a separate drive anyway, then please check out my book "Logic Pro X - Tips, Tricks, Secrets #2" where I have a detailed explanation on how to "outsource" all those sounds to a separate drive using Symbolic Links.

Tracks Window

Flex Pitch Editing Directly on the Track Lane

Flex Pitch Editing in LPX v10.2 was possible on the Track Lane, but only by dragging the Fine Pitch parameter. The extended editing features were only possible in the Audio Track Editor. Now you can use those features and perform the Flex edits directly on the Track Lane without opening the Audio Track Editor.

Keep in mind that the Vertical Zoom Level determines what tools are available (displayed):

▶ **No Flex Pitch**: Even if Flex is enabled ❒ on the Track ❶, you won't see any Flex controls if the vertical zoom level is to low. Only the standard Audio Region ❷ is displayed.

▶ **Basic Flex Pitch**: Once you increase the vertical zoom level high enough, the Note Bars ❸ appear that let you adjust the Fine Pitch.

▶ **Detailed Flex Pitch**: If you increase the zoom level even further, the detailed controls for Flex Pitch appear ❹, the same as the controls in the Audio Track Editor.

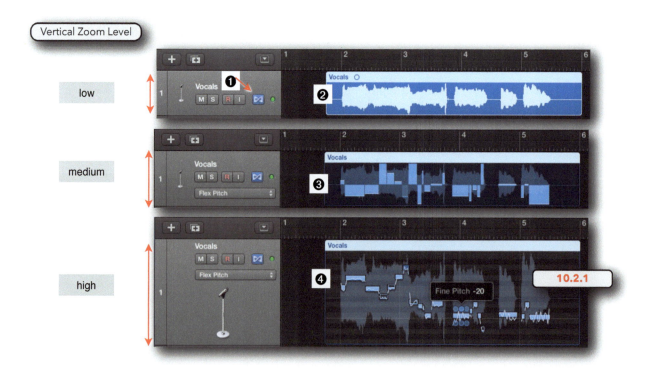

Unique Color for Compressed/Expanded Section in Flexed Audio Region

When you move a Flex Marker on an Audio Region, the section of the waveform to the left and to the right gets expanded or compressed, depending on the direction you move the Flex Marker.

- ▶ **10.2**: The Region Color in those areas became darker ❶ or lighter ❷ to indicate if the section was compressed or expanded.
- ▶ **10.2.1**: Those flexed areas now always have the same color regardless of the Region Color
  - **Gray ❸**: Expanded
  - **White ❹**: Compressed
  - **Red ❺**: Extremely compressed

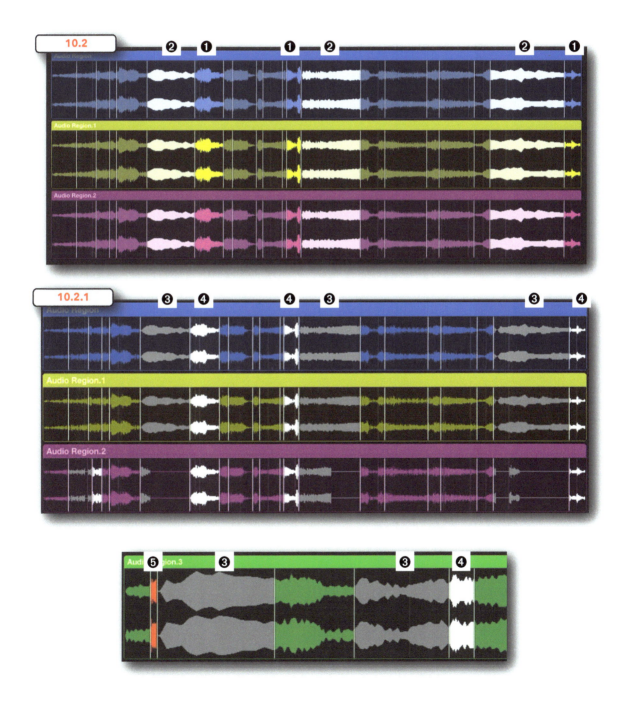

Comp Region Controls Visible when Zoomed and Scrolled

If you are recording using the Take Folder mode, then the top Region represents that Take Folder, a container, also called the Comp Region. Its header displays two elements:

▶ **Controls ❶**: These are the three buttons, the Disclosure Triangle Button, the Take Folder Menu Button, and the Edit Mode Button.

▶ **Names ❷**: The Region Name contains two names, the name of the Comp Region and the name of the Comp.

▶ **10.2**: The problem in LPX v10.2 was that the Comp Region Controls were only displayed at the beginning of the Region ❸. When you moved or scrolled the Workspace and the beginning of the Comp Region was not visible, then you would see only the Comp Region Name, but not the Controls ❹.

▶ **10.2.1**: Now in LPX 10.2.1, the Controls are always visible, together with the Region Name ❺.

Take Folder Menu

There is a minor change in the Take Folder Popup Menu. The previous item "*Flatten (Delete Unused Takes)*" ❻ has been renamed to just "*Flatten*" ❼.

Maybe the "Delete Unused Takes" term was removed, because flattening automatically deletes all the Takes of a Comp (used or unused). However, the Takes are just the "markings" on the individual Take Regions. The Take Regions themselves are not deleted when using the Flatten command.

Suspend Connection Between Arrangement Marker and Regions

The Arrangement Markers ❶ that you create in the Global Arrangement Track automatically connect to the content in the Workspace ❷. Moving (including deleting) any Arrangement Marker will also move its connected content, which are the entire Regions or partial Regions that span between the left and right border of that Arrangement Marker.

Changing the structure of your Song (the Arrangement Marker) without moving the Regions underneath was not possible. Now, LPX v10.2.1 introduces a new mode "**Suspend Content Connection**" that lets you temporarily unlink the Arrangement Marker and the Region Content.

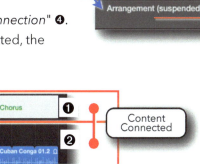

Arrangement Track Header

- ▶ Move the mouse over the Arrangement label ❸ in the Arrangement Track Header.

- ▶ The label reveals a double arrow ⬍ that opens a popup window when you click on it.

- ▶ The only item in that popup menu is "*Suspend Content Connection*" ❹.

- ▶ You can *click* on the menu item to toggle the mode. If selected, the Arrangement label will display (suspended) next to it ❺.

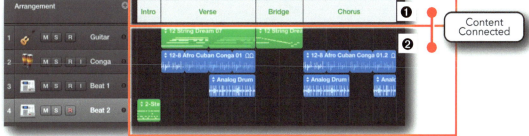

Solo Safe Mode indicated on the Track Header

In LPX 10.2, when a Channel Strip was set to Solo Safe Mode (*ctr+click* on the Solo Button), it indicated that mode with a red line across the button ❻. However, the Solo Button on the Track Header didn't show that red line.

Now in LPX v10.2.1, that Solo Safe Button is also displayed in the Track Header ❼.

Please note that you cannot enable/disable Solo Safe Mode on the Track Header's Solo Button ❼. *Ctr+click* only works on the Channel Strip ❻.

Flex Time Edits on grouped Phase-Locked Audio Regions

In LPX v10.2, when you have Audio Tracks assigned to a Group ❶ and enable "Editing" ❷ plus "Phase-Locked Audio" ❸ for that Group, then the Track Header on those Track displays the Q-Reference Button ❹. All those Regions edits are now performed as a group. However, if Flex Time ❺ is enabled on those Tracks to perform "grouped" Flex Edits ❻ on those Regions, then those Regions had to have the same start time. If their start time was just a few frames off, then you got an error message ❼.

New

In LPX 10.2.1, the Regions on those grouped Tracks can now have different start positions and that Alert window will not pop up anymore.

Now up to 500 Custom Icons

LPX v10.2 introduced the ability to add your own Custom Icons (*ctr+click* on the Icon in the Track Header and select "Custom Icons" ❽). However, the number of Custom Icons was limited to 100.

Now in LPX 10.2.1, that limit has been raised to 500.

Those icons are stored in the user directory **~/Music/Audio Music Apps/Custom Icons/** ❾.

For all the details and hidden functionality refer to my book "Logic Pro X - How it Works" (p. 151) and "Logic Pro X - Trips, Tricks, Secrets #1" (p. 44).

Tracks Icon Window

New Alchemy Track Icon

There is also a new Track Icon ❶ available in the Keyboard category ❷ of the Track Icons window that is selected as a default when you load the Alchemy Plugin ❸ on a Software Instrument Channel Strip .

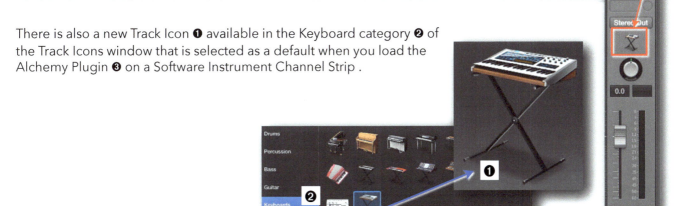

New Region from Capture Recording is selected

When you record a MIDI Region and hit stop, then the newly created Region is automatically selected. However, when using the Capture Recording ❹ feature (Key Command *sh+R*), the newly created MIDI Region was not automatically selected.

Now in LPX 10.2.1, it is.

Capture Recording (MIDI)

Vertical Help Line reaches all the way to the Bar Ruler

In LPX 10.2, when you drag or resize a Region in the Workspace, a vertical Help Line ❺ spanned across the Workspace to better align it against other Regions.

Now in LPX 10.2.1, this Help Line reaches across the Global Tracks ❻ all the way to the Ruler ❼ on top (which it didn't do before).

Please not that this Help Line is different from the yellow Alignment Guides that you can activate from the Snaps Menu (or Key Command *opt+cmd+G*). When enabled, it turns the white Help Line yellow when it "encounters" a Region border on another Track.

Tracks Window

Beat Mapping Improvements

The Beat Mapping feature has a function that automatically creates the Beat Mapping for an existing Audio File. On the Track Header of the Global Beat Mapping Track (toggle with **sh +cmd+B**) click on the "Beat Mapping" ❶ label and select "*Beats from Region*" ❷ from the popup menu. This opens a Dialog window that lets you select the Note Values ❸ for the mapping and the algorithm ❹.

Tracks Window ➤ Beat Mapping

Here are the improvements:

▶ **New Algorithms**: LPX 10.2.1 has improved the algorithms for the "Beats from Region" ❷ function, which should deliver a correct Beat Mapping result for most Audio Files.

▶ **Hints**: The algorithm will use "hints" to improve the results of the "*Beats from Region*" process.

- Any transients that are mapped manually to a bar or beat will be taken into account as "hints" when LPX performs the automatic Beat Mapping with "*Beats from Region*" process. Just map a few transients manually prior to the "*Beats from Region*" process to improve the results.

- If the results of the "*Beats from Region*" process is not perfect, then adding a few more hints (manually mapped transients) might help.

- Manually mapping transients before or after a section of silence in the Audio File will also be taken into account as "hints".

- The Time Signature in the Control Bar Display will also be taken into account.

Also Added: Beat Mapping now also works with Take Regions.

Improved Waveform Display

The waveform display of an Audio Region on the Track Lane has been optimized. It is now more accurate at a lower zoom level.

Issues with the waveform display when zooming out vertically have also been fixed.

Here are two screenshots of the same Audio Region displayed in LPX 10.2 and LPX 10.2.1.

Key Signature Displayed in the Custom LCD

The Custom Toolbar Display ⚙ has a new component "**Key Signature**" ❶ that can be displayed next to the Time Signature.

A few things to know:

▶ *Ctr+Click* on the Toolbar background to open a Popover displaying a checkbox ❷ in the LCD section (disabled by default) to make the Key Signature visible.

▶ *Click* on the Key Signature in the LCD to open a popup menu ❸ that lets you select a different Key Signature.

▶ Unlike the Time Signature, which only lets you enter a value on the LCD, if you don't have Time Signature changes in your Project, you can change the Key Signature any time and it will be entered at the current Playhead Position.

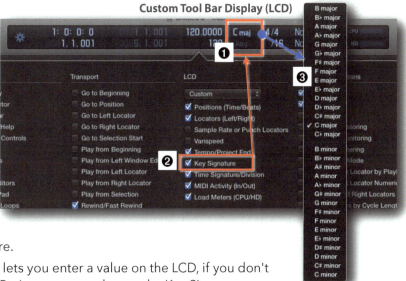

Custom Tool Bar Display (LCD)

Help Tags with Region Length Info

Now, when you *click-hold* on a Region, the Help Tag displays the Length ❹ of that Region in addition to Position and Track info.

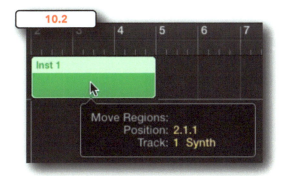

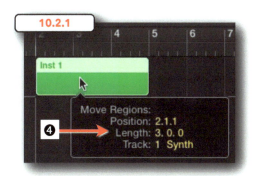

Background Tasks as Progress Bar on LCD

Here is a little undocumented change in LPX 10.2.1 that can be easily overlooked.

Usually, apps display a small window with a progress bar that indicates the progress of an ongoing task. In Logic, that could be indexing Apple Loops, creating waveform overviews, or the download of additional sound content from Apple. Some of those tasks take priority, which means, you have to wait until they are completed before you can continue in Logic.

LPX 10.2.1 made the following changes:

- ☑ Tasks can now run in the background without interrupting your work in Logic
- ☑ The progress window will not pop up in your face anymore
- ☑ A little Progress Bar ❶ appears on the Display Mode Button on the far left of the Control Bar Display (LCD) to indicate an ongoing task
- ☑ You can *click* on the Progress Bar to open a Popover Window displaying additional information if available

Control Bar Display

Here are some of the Background Tasks displayed in the LCD:

● Indexing Apple Loops

The indexing of Apple Loops was a really annoying one. The Progress Window ❷ didn't show a real time progression and you had to wait until it was finished, which could take some time for bigger Apple Loops Libraries. Now, it indexes in the background without interruption (except the Loop Browser). However, the progress bar still doesn't give you a proper time indication ❸.

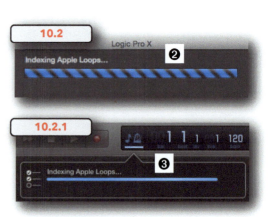

● Creating Waveform Overview

When you import audio files into your Project, Logic creates an overview of the waveform for those audio files to be displayed on the audio region. In LPX 10.2, a separate Progress Window pops up ❹ with a progress bar and time indicators to inform you about the progress. A checkbox "Faster overview..." lets you speed up the calculation process.

The new Popover Window ❺ shows the same information. In addition, you can cancel the process with the X-button ❻ [X], but the checkmarks ❼ on the left are just decoration and are not active click buttons.

● Downloading Library Sound Content

Although the downloading of additional library content was a background task before, now the Popover Window ❽ provides more detailed information on what is currently downloaded, plus the size and time estimates. In addition, you see all the individual packages lined up in a queue ❾ (Idle), what is downloaded next. The Pause Button ❿ [II] lets you interrupt the download (then, continue or cancel), or you can cancel any individual download with the x-button [X].

Import Tempo Information from a MIDI File

Logic can import any tempo information that is included as Metadata in an audio file. Now in version 10.2.1, it can also import the embedded tempo information of a MIDI file when you import it into your Project.

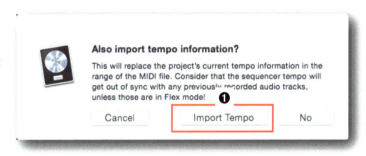

A Dialog Window pops up up during the import giving you the option to "**Import Tempo**" ❶.

Import Tempo Map from Music Memos

 Apple just released a new iOS app called "**Music Memos**". It lets you quickly record your musical ideas on your iPhone wherever you are. Automatically synced to your iCloud account, when you are back in the studio or on your MacBook, you can quickly import those audio files into your Logic Project.

The app is super easy to use with some amazing features. Some Logic related notes:

- ▸ **File Format**: The audio files are recorded in 24bit - 44.1kHz - mono - CAF (Core Audio Format).
- ▸ **iCloud Sync**: Once you recorded an audio file on the iPhone, it will be synced to iCloud and show up on your computer. Select "Cloud Drive" ❷ in the Finder's Sidebar and open the "Music Memos" ❸ folder. You can rename the files in the Finder (updated on your iPhone's Music Memos app).
- ▸ **Import**: Just drag the audio file into Logic.
- ▸ **Import Tempo**: If this is a new Project without any Tempo changes in the Tempo Track, you will be prompted with a Dialog Window ❹ to choose if you want to import the Tempo Map that is embedded in the audio file. The downbeat of the audio file automatically snaps to the closest bar.
- ▸ **Tempo + Key + Time Signature**: When you choose "Import", Logic creates not only Tempo Events ❺ based on the tempo map from the audio file, but also Key Signature ❻ and Time Signature ❼ Events.
- ▸ **Import Later**: Like with any other Audio File, you can import the embedded Information of an Audio File at any time later by using the Main Menu command *Edit ➤ Tempo ➤ Import Tempo Information from Audio File*. This command also imports the Key Signature and Time Signature.

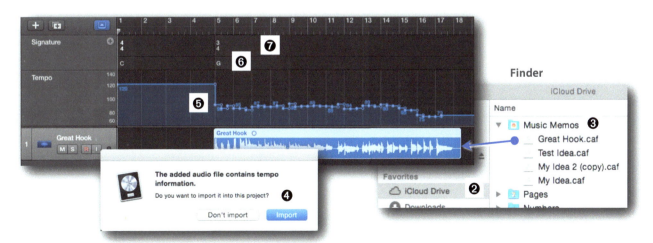

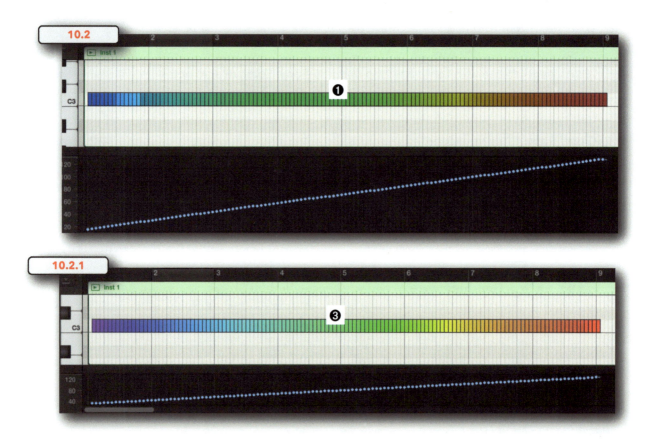

Piano Roll Editor

Extended Range for the Velocity Color of Note Events

The Note Events in the Piano Roll Editor are color coded indicating their different velocity values ❶. This is the default behavior set in the Piano Roll's Local Menu *View ➤ Set Note Color ➤ By Velocity* ❷.

Now in LPX 10.2.1, the range of the colors representing the velocity values 1-127 has been extended ❸.

Piano Roll Editor: View Menu

New "Region Transpose" in Piano Roll's Local View Menu

The Region Inspector has a Transpose Parameter ❶ that lets you transpose all Note Events of a Region by a value between -96 and +96 semitones (8 octaves). However, this is a so-called Playback Parameter that does not change the actual pitch of the Notes when displayed in the MIDI Editors ❷.

Now the Piano Roll's Local View Menu has an additional item, "Region Transpose" ❹. When selected, it displays the Note Events with the applied transpose value ❸.

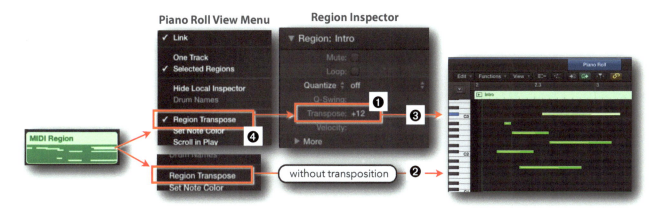

Addition to the Snap Menu

The Snap Menu ❺ in the Piano Roll has two additional commands ❻:

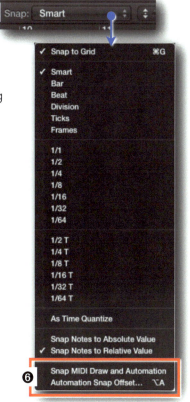

▸ **Snap MIDI Draw and Automation**: When enabled, all the Control Points for Automation Parameters and MIDI Draw Parameters snap to the grid value set in the Snap Menu.

▸ **Automation Snap Offset...**: This opens the *Preferences ➤ Automation* window to set the Snap Offset for Automation Control Points (including MIDI Draw Control Points) between -99 and +99 ticks.

One minor detail: The triplet values in the Snap Menu are now displayed differently.

"Tempo" submenu removed in the Piano Roll's local Edit menu

The local Edit Menu in the Piano Roll had a Tempo submenu ❶. In case you wondered, that menu has been removed ❷ in LPX v10.2.1, because those commands didn't apply to the Piano Roll Editor anyway.

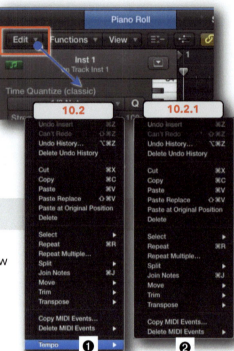

Add MIDI Draw data in any Region

LPX v10.2 had an annoying bug where you could only enter MIDI Draw data in the first Region in the Piano Roll Editor when multiple Regions were displayed.

Now in LPX v10.2.1, you can draw in any Region ❸ in the MIDI Draw Area.

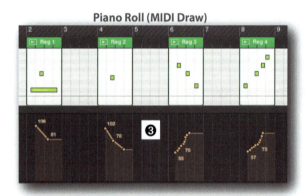

Piano Roll (MIDI Draw)

Long-click with Quantize Tool opens Quantize Menu (again)

Another bug in the Piano Roll has been fixed in LPX 10.2.1.

Now, when you *long-click* with the Quantize Tool on a Note Event ❹ in the Piano Roll, a popup menu displays all the Quantize values ❺ to select from.

This is the same behavior when *long-clicking* with the Quantize Tool on a Note in the Score Editor.

Piano Roll Editor

3 - New Features in the Main Window

Sh+ctr+click to Insert Notes without the Snap Restriction

The Snap value set in the Piano Roll not only has an effect when moving or resizing Note Events, it also restricts the position of newly created notes to the selected Snap Grid.

▸ **_Click_** with Pencil Tool ✎: This creates a new Note Event that snaps to the nearest time grid based on the current Snap Value ❶.

▸ **_Sh+ctr+click_** with Pencil Tool ✎: This creates a new Note Event at the exact click position ❷, ignoring the current Snap setting.

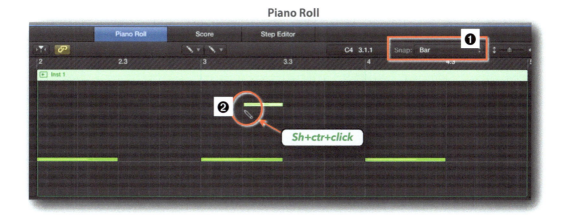

Flip Time Handles Area

When you enable Time Handle Mode in the Piano Roll by selecting it in the Local Menu **_Functions ➤ Time Handle_** ❸, you can draw a range (time frame) in the Notes Area and drag the left or right Time Handles ❹ on top to time compress/expand those Note Events. There is a special behavior when you drag the Time Handles past another that has changed:

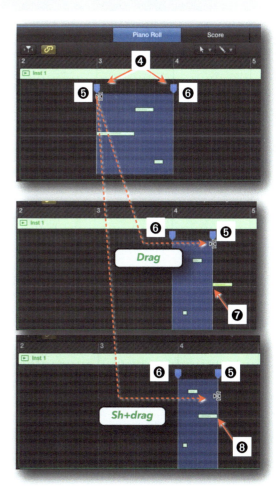

▸ **_Drag_**: In this example, I drag the left Time Handle ❺ to the right, past the right Time Handle ❻. The Handle keeps the "Compress Left Border Tool" ▤ to indicate that this is the original left border. The movement pivots the notes start position ❼ in addition to any compression/expansion, depending on how far you drag.

▸ **_Sh+drag_**: This is the 10.2 behavior where the movement swaps the note starts and ends ❽.

You can actually press or release the shift key while dragging to see one or the other behavior before releasing the mouse. It is best to play around a little to get the hang of it.

Staff Styles Window displays Colors in Note Menu

The Staff Styles Window ❶ in the Score Editor lets you set a specific Note Head color for each Voice in a Staff. You **click** on the Color field ❷ and select the color from the popup menu.

In LPX v10.2, the menu only listed the Color Number 0 ... 15 ❸. Now in LPX v10.2.1, the menu also shows the actual color ❹ that represents that number, which is also shown in the Color Field of the Staff Styles Window ❷.

These 16 colors are defined in *Project Settings ➤ Score ➤ Color* in the "User Palette" ❺.

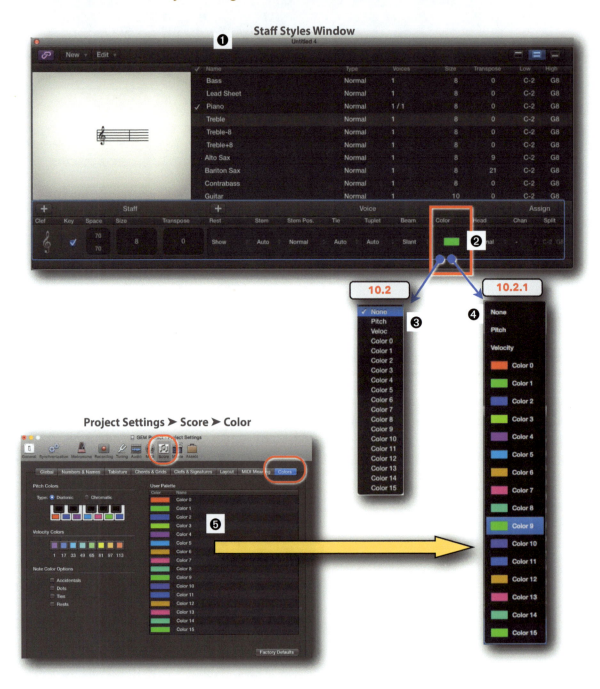

3 - New Features in the Main Window

Edit Size and Transposition numerically in the Staff Style Window

The standard procedure for editing numeric values in Logic is to *click-drag* on the number to slide its value up/down or to *double-click* on the number, type a new number, and hit enter.

The two numeric values for Size ❶ and Transpose ❷ in the Staff Style Window (*sh+ctr+op+S*) of the Score Editor couldn't be edited by typing in a new number. Now in LPX 10.2.1, it works.

Once, you *double-click* on the number, it turns blue ❸ (to indicate it has key focus), and you can enter a new numeric value.

Staff Style Window

Active Group in Part Box indicated by a Frame

Opening the Score Editor (so it has key focus) will show the Part Box ❹ in the Main Inspector. You can select multiple group buttons, which are marked as blue ❺, to display their symbols below.

In LPX 10.2.1, when selecting any individual symbol ❻ (turns blue) in the Part box, it will have a frame around the group button ❼ the selected symbol belongs to.

Main Inspector: Part Box

New Setting to "Hide First" Time Signature

Project Settings ➤ Score ➤ Clefs & Signatures

The *Project Settings ➤ Score ➤ Clefs & Signatures ➤ Time Signatures* ❽ has a new item in the popup menu, "**Hide First**"❾. It will hide the very first Time Signature in your Score.

Also, the "Hide All" Time Signatures project setting now hides all time signatures as expected.

Smooth Pinch Gesture to Zoom in-out of Score Window

BTW, if you don't use a trackpad (yet) to zoom in and out of the Score Editor (or most of the other windows), then you are missing out big time on one of the most important workflow enhancements I can think of in Logic. Now in LPX 10.2.1, the zooming is super responsive.

Double-click in the Score Set to Create new Instrument Entry

To add a new line (Instrument) in the Score Set Window, you had to use the Local Menu Command *New ➤ Add Instrument Entry* ❶. Now in LPX 10.2.1 you can also just *double-click* ❷ in the Instrument Area below the last line to create an entry for the next Instrument (like it was done in Logic Pro 9).

Improved Behavior for Folder Regions in Link Modes

This is a very specific improvement that you only can appreciate (and understand) if you have a good understanding of the Score Editor and the use of the Score Editor and Folder Regions.

 Same Level Link

▸ **Select a <u>Region</u> in the Workspace**: The Score Editor switches the Instrument/Score Set Filter to the Instrument (Track) of that Region, displaying all the Regions on that Track.

▸ **Select a Region <u>Folder</u> in the Workspace**: The behavior has changed.
   - 10.2: The Score Editor doesn't switch the Filter and potentially doesn't display anything.
   - 10.2.1: The Score Editor switches the Instrument/Score Set Filter to "All Instrument", properly displaying all Tracks for those Regions and the Regions on those Tracks.

 **Content Link**

▸ **Select a <u>Region</u> in the Workspace**: The Score Editor displays the selected Region in Single Region Mode ignoring the current Score Set Filter, which will not change.

▸ **Select a Region <u>Folder</u> in the Workspace**: The Score Editor displays the content of the selected Region using the current Score Set Filter. If the current Filter would result in an empty display, then the behavior is now different:
   - 10.2: The Score Editor displays nothing.
   - 10.2.1: The Score Editor switches the Filter to "All Instruments" and properly displays the content of the selected Folder.

Audio File Editor: New Vertical Zoom Behavior

When you zoom vertically on the waveform of a stereo audio file in the Audio File Editor, you will notice a different behavior in LPX v10.2.1:

▶ **10.2**: The Audio File Editor is centered around the border between the left and right waveform ❶. When you zoom in, that center stays fixed, which means the left (top) and right (bottom) waveform zooming "out of sight", because now you see only the bottom of the left waveform ❷ and the top of the right waveform ❸.

▶ **10.2.1**: Now when zooming in, the center stays around the 0-line of the left (top) waveform ❹. That means that the right (bottom) waveform gradually disappears ❺, while zooming in further into the left waveform ❻.

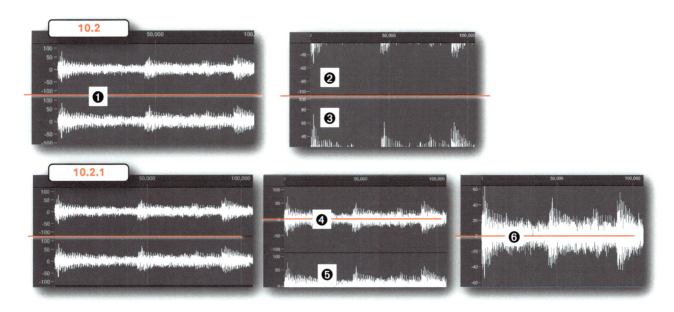

Zoom Slider Position in Order

Here is a little change that is not really ground-breaking, but demonstrates the attention to detail (or the "sense of order" shown by the German Logic team).

▶ **10.2**: The placement of the horizontal and vertical Zoom Slider in the Audio File Editor didn't follow the same order as in the Tracks Window.

▶ **10.2.1**: Now this "eye sore" has been fixed and the vertical Zoom Slider is first ❼ and the Horizontal Zoom Slider is ❽ to the right like in the Tracks Window, the Piano Roll Editor, or the Step Editor.

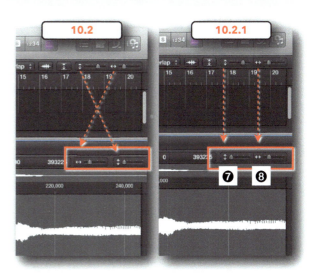

Playhead stays visible in the Audio File Editor

This little improvement has a big impact for editing audio in the Audio File Editor.

- ▶ **10.2.0**: The Playhead is only visible in the Audio File Editor during playback. When you stop playback, the Playhead disappears.
- ▶ **10.2.1**: Now, the Playhead stays visible ❶ in the Audio File Editor and can be used for audio editing.

Audio File Editor

Editing in the Audio File Editor with the Playhead

Now that the Playhead stays visible in the Audio File Editor, audio editing becomes better.

- ▶ *Drag* the Playhead Thumb ❷ (the top of the Playhead in the Ruler) to scrub the audio.
- ▶ The Prelisten Button ❸ on the Menu Bar turns green during scrubbing and the Cursor Tool will display a speaker icon on top of the Playhead.
- ▶ *Dragging* the Playhead when only a Selection Line ❹ is selected, will move the Selection Line to the Playhead Position ❺ when releasing the mouse.
- ▶ *Sh+dragging* the Playhead when a Selection Area ❻ is selected, will extend the Selection Area to the Playhead Position on the right or left of the Selection Area, depending on where you are scrubbing.

Auto-zoom in to the Full Waveform

The following improvement was listed in the Release Notes, but I couldn't make it work on my setup.

- 💡 *The Audio File editor now zooms to use the full horizontal width of the screen when you double-click an audio region.*

Set Multiple Events to the Same Value

The click action to set multiple selected Events to the same value using the modifier keys *shift+option* already existed in 10.2, however, you had to *click-hold* on the value first and then press the modifier keys.

In LPX v10.2.1, the procedure is more straightforward:

- ☑ Select the Events you want to change.
- ☑ Press down the modifier keys *shift+option* first.
- ☑ *Clicking* on any value of the selected Events (i.e. Velocity value), will set the value of all the selected Events to that value.
- ☑ You can also drag the value up/down (while holding down the *sh+opt* keys) to change those values together.

Here is an example with 5 selected Note Events. *Sh+opt+clicking* on the Velocity value 42 ❶ of one of the Events will change all those values to 42 ❷. *Sh+opt+click* on the Velocity value 117 ❸ of one of the Events will change all those values to 117 ❹.

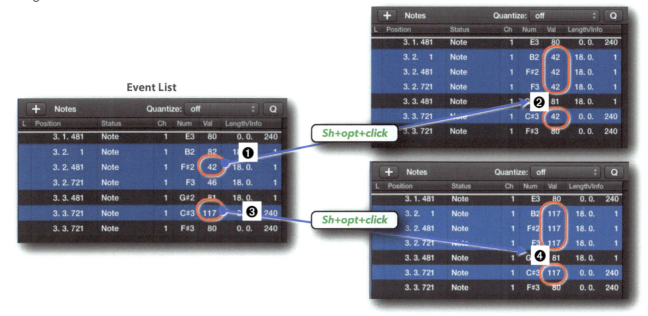

Opt+click to Play Solo

Opt+click-hold on an Event in the Event List starts the Solo Play from that Event. The Cursor Tool changes to the Solo Tool ❺ when pressing down the option key to indicate this function.

Now in LPX v10.2.1, when you press the option key, the Solo Tool only appears when you hover the mouse over the Status column ❻ in the Event List.

Drag All Selected Events to minimum and maximum Value

There are different behaviors for changing the values of multiple selected Events in the Event List by dragging the numbers up or down.

⚉ Group Limit

This is the default behavior. When you select multiple Events ❶ in the Event List, you *click-drag* on one value ❷ up or down and all the selected Events will change their value together proportionally. However, you can slide up or down the value only until one of the groups of selected Events reaches its maximum or minimum value. That's why I call this "Group Limit", because there is one max and min value for the entire group of selected Events.

⚉ Individual Limit

You can use the *option* key to change the behavior to what I call an "Individual Limit", which means, each Event in the group of selected Events can be pushed to the maximum or minimum value.

Event List

You have to follow the exact procedure with this modifier key:

- ☑ Select the Events first.
- ☑ *Click-hold* on one number (in the Val field).
- ☑ While holding down the mouse and dragging up or down, press down the *option* key ❸.
- ☑ Any value that reaches the minimum or maximum value remains there while you are still dragging the value of the one Event you clicked, until it reaches that limit too. That means, the Events lose their proportional value and are set to the same min or max value. This is a quick way to set a group of Events to the same value, for example, the same Velocity.
- ☑ However, here is an important little detail: You have to drag the smallest value in the group up to move all values to 127, or move the biggest value down to move all values to 1.

▶ **10.2.1**: The Individual Limit procedure didn't work for the maximum value in 10.2, but now it works for the minimum and maximum value.

Event Type Popup Menu with added Fader Event

The Event Type popup menu ❹ lets you select the type of MIDI Event that gets added to the currently selected Region at the Playhead Position when you click the Plus Button ❺ ➕.

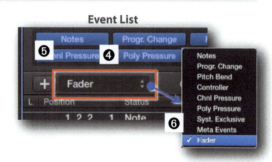

Event List

▶ **10.2.1**: Now, the popup menu also lists the Fader ❻ Event Type, so you can add Automation Data directly in the Event List.

"Automatic" option in the Lane Set Popup Menu

When you select the Step Editor Window, the Main Inspector will show two sections, the Lane Inspector ❶ and the Lane Set Popup Menu ❷.

Clicking on the Lane Set Popup Menu opens , you guessed it, a popup menu ❸. It contains all the commands related to the Lane Sets in the Step Editor. There is one new menu item "Automatic" ❹, on top of the menu.

➡ *Automatic Lane Set*

In the Step Editor Window, each MIDI type (notes, controller type, etc.) is displayed in a separate Lane ❺. But in order to display the MIDI Events in their Lanes, you have to create a Lane Set first that contains the corresponding Lane. In LPX 10.2, there were two Lane Sets ❻ that automatically created a Lane Set, "MIDI Controls" and "GM Drum Kit". Now the new "Automatic" ❹ Lane Set also creates a Lane Set automatically, but the difference is that it creates a Lane Set dynamically. Here is how it works:

> 💡 Instead of manually creating a Lane Set, just select "Automatic" and the Step Editor will display a Lane Set with a separate Lane for each MIDI Event type in the currently selected Region. This way, you don't have to worry about which Event Types are contained in a specific MIDI Region. Logic will display the correct Lanes, and updates them dynamically. That means, if you add another Event Type, i.e. add Breath Controller, Logic will automatically add a Lane for the Breath Controller type (CC2). Removing a specific MIDI Type from the Region (i.e. all Modulation data) will remove the Lane for CC1 from the Lane Set.

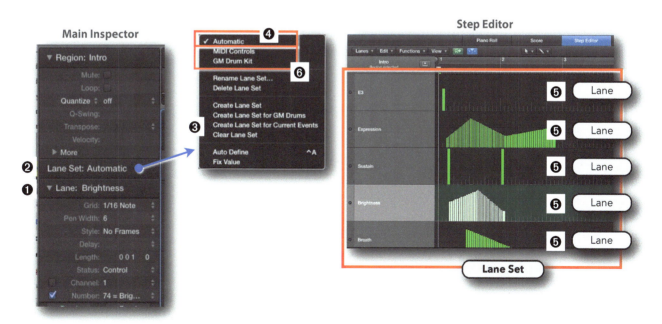

Attention: It seems that the "Automatic" Lane Set won't be displayed when opening a Project saved in Logic Projects prior to LPX v10.2.1.

"Go To Position" Window Bug Fixed

When you re-open the Go To Position Window (Key Command /), the **New** Position field ❻ should remember the position you entered the last time when the window was open (which is useful as a Memory Locator).

LPX 10.2 had a bug where this New Position was always overwritten with the Current Position when you opened this window. This is now fixed in LPX 10.2.1 and works as expected.

Individual Catch Playhead Mode for each Window

While the implementation of the Catch Playhead feature stayed the same, the way a specific mode is selected has changed:

▶ In the *Preferences ➤ General ➤ Catch*, you set the default Catch Playhead Mode by enabling/disabling the three checkboxes ❶. This will be the default Catch Playhead status for all newly opened windows that have a Catch Playhead Button [icon] on their Menu Bar.

▶ Now, each window with a Catch Playhead Button [icon] can be changed to a different Catch Playhead mode individually. *Ctr-click* on the Catch Playhead Button to open its new Shortcut Menu ❷ that lists the three Catch options. Select or deselect the items by clicking on them.

▶ The individual Catch Playhead settings on a window are remembered with the Screensets. This way, you can switch between different Catch Playhead Modes on the same window by switching Screensets.

Preferences ➤ General ➤ Catch

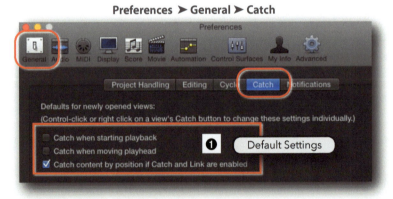

Remember: The Key Command (*Catch Playhead Position*) ` (the key above the "tab" key) lets you quickly toggle the Catch Playhead Button on/off.

New Modifier Keys for Resizing Markers

There are two new modifier key actions in LPX v10.2.1 for resizing a Marker. Here are the modifier keys that change the Pointer Tool:

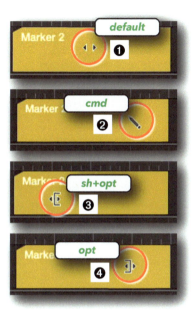

▶ **❶ Move Marker** ◁ ▷: This is the default Tool, when moving the Pointer Tool over a Marker. *Drag* the Marker to move it. *Double-click* with that Tool to open the name field to change the Marker name.

▶ **❷ Create New Marker** ✎: Holding down the command key when the Pointer Tool is over the Marker Track switches to the Pencil Tool. *Cmd +click* to create a new Marker at that click position.

▶ **❸ Resize Left Border** ◀Ɛ *NEW*: Holding down the shift and option key when the Pointer Tool is over a Marker switches to the Resize Left Tool. *Sh+opt+click* (or drag) on an existing Marker to set the beginning to that click position. The left border of a Marker functions as a Click Zone that automatically switches the Cursor Tool to the Left Resize Tool.

▶ **❹ Resize Right Border** Ɛ▶ *NEW*: *Opt+click* (or drag) on an existing Marker to set the end to that click position or *Opt+drag* the right border. The right border of a Marker functions as a Click Zone that automatically switches the Pointer Tool to the Left Resize Tool.

▶ *Attention*: If you want to copy a Marker, then you have to *click-hold* on the Marker and then hold the *option* key before *dragging*.

Wrapped Marker Name

There is a small change to how the Marker Name is displayed in the Global Marker Track. To better understand that, you have to be aware that a Marker can have two text components:

▶ **Marker Name**: This is the single-line text you entered when you name a Marker in the Marker Track or the Marker List. In the Marker Text Area of the Marker List or the standalone Marker Text Window, this would be the first line.

▶ **Additional Text**: In the Marker Text Area of the Marker List or the standalone Marker Text Window, you can enter more than one line of text using the *return* key. This way you can enter additional text similar to a text editor. This additional text can be displayed if the Marker Track is increased vertically.

Here is the change to how the Marker Name is displayed on the Marker Track if the name is longer than the Marker (depending on the horizontal zoom):

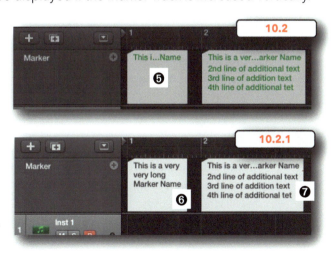

💡 **10.2**: The Marker Name is truncated if there is not enough space ❺.

💡 **10.2.1**: It depends on the following condition:

• If the Marker has no additional text, then the Marker Name will be wrapped to the next line(s) ❻, displaying it in full.

• If the Marker has additional text, then the Marker Name (the first line) is truncated ❼. Additional text will always be wrapped to the next line if necessary.

Global Tempo Track - New Click Behavior

The click behavior has changed in the Global Tempo Track Lane to conform to the click behavior in the Automation Lane:

- ▶ **10.2**: *Click* on the Tempo Curve to select that Tempo Curve segment
- ▶ **10.2.1**: *Click* on the Tempo Curve to create a new Control Point

The Global Tempo Track has a ton of click actions. Let me, as a bonus, list all those actions (I'm sure there are a few more that I missed) to refresh your memory:

➡ *Terminology*

A few things you have to be aware of:

- ▶ Those dots that represent a single Tempo Event have different names depending upon who you ask or what book you read: For example, *Tempo Points*, *Automation Points*, or *Nodes*. I use Control Points.

- ▶ A Control Point always presents the segment of the Tempo Curve up to the next Control Point; therefore, a Control Point and its segment are always selected together.

- ▶ There are also hollow Control Points that let you change the shape of the Tempo Curve by dragging them around. They create additional (hidden) Control Points that can be made visible in the Tempo List Window by clicking on the "Additional Info" button.

➡ *Click Actions*

🔘 Select Control Point

- *Click-hold* on a Control Point or line.
- *Sh+click* on a Control Point or a line. An already selected Control Point will be de-selected.
- *Sh+double-click* on a Control Point or a line to open the Tempo List Window.
- *Drag* around an area of the Tempo Curve (lasso around) to select all the Control Points inside.
- *Sh+drag* around an area of the Tempo Curve to add the selection to an existing selection. Dragging over already selected Control Points will de-select those Control Points.

- *Click* on the Tempo Track Header to select all Control Points.
- *Sh+click* on the Tempo Track Header to toggle the selection of the Control Points.
- *Click* in the Track Lane (not on a curve) to de-select all Control Points. Be careful, if you click too close to the Tempo Curve, you will create a new Control Point.

🔘 Create a Control Point

- *Click* on the Tempo Curve.
- *Double-click* anywhere on the Tempo Track to create a Control Point at that point.
- *Click* anywhere on the Tempo Track with the Pencil Tool 🖊 to create a Control Point at that point.

🔘 Change Control Point

- *Drag* a Control Point, a single Tempo Curve segment, or a group of selected Tempo Curve segments.
- *Sh+drag* a Control Point to limit to a horizontal movement. This will also let you move without a grid.
- *Ctr+drag* vertically lets you move vertically with a finer resolution (2 decimals). Watch the Help Tag.
- *Sh+ctr+drag* vertically lets you move vertically with an even finer resolution (4 decimal). Watch the Help Tag.

🔘 Delete Control Points

- *Double+click* on a Control Point.
- *Click* on a Control Point with the Eraser Tool 🖊.

New Splitter Icon to Adjust Height of Global Tracks

This new "feature" is not as quite as earth-shattering, but it was mentioned in the Release Notes and I thought I should point it out, to at least acknowledge the effort that someone on the Logic team implemented (for whatever reason).

Tracks Window

: The Cursor Tool changes to this Tool ❶ when you move it on the divider line between Tracks to vertically resize them by dragging up or down.

: The Cursor Tool changes to this Tool ❷ when you move it on the divider line between Global Tracks to vertically resize them by dragging up or down. The exception is the divider line on the lowest Global Track, which changes to the other Resize Tool ❸ and resizes all visible Global Tracks proportionally.

Menu Bar Controls Move to the Action Menu

When you decrease the width of the Main Window and there is not enough space for all the controls on the Menu Bar, then some of the controls ❹ will be moved one by one as menu items to an Action Menu Button ❺ that appears on the Menu Bar.

> ▶ **10.2**: Only the Snap Menu ❻ and the Drag Menu ❼ were moved to the Action Menu.
> ▶ **10.2.1**: Now, the Catch Playhead Button ❽, the Vertical Auto Zoom Button ❾, and the Waveform Zoom Button ❿ also move to the Action Menu if there is not enough space on the Menu Bar.

Main Window

The Tool Menu Button will also disappear if there is not enough space, but they will not be listed in the Action Menu.

Double-click on Audio File in Project Browser

This is a minor change in the Project Browser:

 10.2: *Double-clicking* on an Audio File (the waveform) in the Project Audio Browser opens the Audio File Editor as a standalone window.

 10.2.1: *Double-clicking* on an Audio File (the waveform) in the Project Audio Browser ❶ opens the Audio File Editor in the Editors Pane ❷ of Logic's Main Window. *Double-clicking* on an Audio File (the waveform) in the standalone Project Audio Window ❸ opens the Audio File Editor as a standalone window ❹.

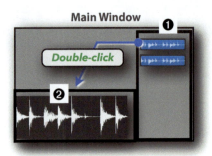
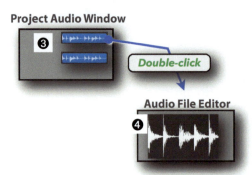

Note Pad: Limited Fonts Panel

When opening the Fonts Panel by *clicking* on the A button ❺ in the Note Pad Window, you will have less ❻ format buttons in the Font Panel's Toolbar than you had in LPX v10.2 ❼.

I admit, that change is not that dramatic.

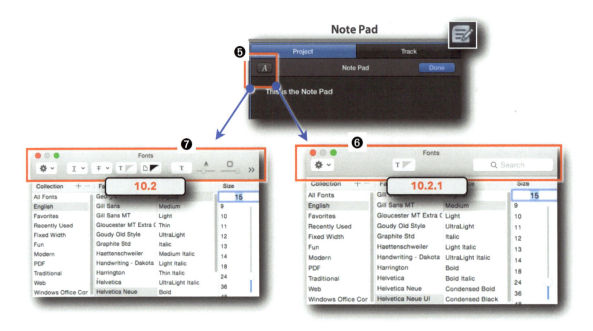

Inspector

Clicking on the VCA Slot displays the VCA Channel Strip on the right

The two Channel Strips in the Main Inspector provide a great functionality that was expanded in v10.2.1. While the left Inspector Channel Strip displays the assigned Channel Strip of the currently selected Track, the right Channel Strip depends on what you clicked on in the left Channel Strip.

▸ **Output Channel Strip** (default) ❶: *Clicking* on the Output Button on the left Channel Strip will display the Output Channel Strip for that output bus.

▸ **Aux Channel Strip** ❷: *Clicking* on any Send Button on the left Channel Strip displays the Aux Channel Strip that uses that Send Bus as its input.

▸ **VCA Master Fader** *(NEW)* ❸: *Clicking* on an assigned VCA Slot displays the corresponding VCA Channel Strip.

Output Channel Strip

Aux Channel Strip

VCA Channel Strip

Multiple Group Selection and Settings Editing in Group Inspector

The Groups Inspector is the window displayed in the Main Inspector that provides all the settings for configuring the individual Channel Strip Groups. 10.2.1 adds the following new functionality:

- ▶ Now you can select multiple Groups in the list ❹ to edit the settings for all those Groups together. Use the standard select procedures *sh+click* (select contiguous Groups) or *cmd+click* (select non-contiguous Groups).

- ▶ A checkbox will show a hyphen ❺ to indicate that some of the selected Groups have this checkbox selected and some deselected.

"Assign Channel Strip Color..." now works in the Inspector Channel Strip

To assign a Channel Strip Color ❶ (which is also used on the related Track), you *ctr+click* on the Channel Strip background ❷ and select "*Assign Channel Strip Color…*" from the Shortcut Menu ❸. This opens the Color Palette ❹ where you *click* on a color ❺ to apply it to the currently selected Channel Strip(s). Make sure, no Region is selected at the time.

Although this Shortcut Menu ❺ was also available in the Inspector Channel Strip, the command didn't work.

Now, in LPX 10.2.1 it works.

Inspector Channel Strip

Automation

Blue is the new Yellow

The following Automation buttons have changed from yellow to blue:

- **Show/Hide Automation**: Old , new
- **Enable Track Automation**: Old Track , new Track
- **Enable Region Automation**: Old Region , new Region

➡ *Flex Turned Blue Too*

The two buttons for Flex Modes have also changed to blue from their previous purple color.

- **Show/Hide Flex**: Old , new
- **Enable Flex**: Old , new

Colored Automation Mode Buttons on the Track Header

In LPX v10.2, all the Automation Mode Buttons on the Track Header were gray. Now, they have the same color as the corresponding buttons on the Channel Strip.

Three things I want to point out:

- The special green font on the gray button Read ⬍ means that Read Automation is enabled, but no Automation data (no Control Points) have been created on that Track yet. This is the default status on a Track.

- The gray buttons indicate that Automation is disabled on that Track. On the Track Header you toggle that status with the Power

Button on the Track Automation Button ⏻ Trk and Region Automation Button ⏻ Rgn . On the Channel Strip, the Power Button is part of the Automation Mode Button ⏻ Read ⬍ itself when you move the Pointer Tool over it.

- The Trim-Write option doesn't exist for apparent reasons.

If you are still struggling with the Automation feature in Logic, please check out my manual "Logic Pro X - The Details", the only book that explains all the automation features in Logic on over 100 pages.

Automation Curve displayed in Collapsed Track Stack

Now in LPX 10.2.1 when you collapse a Track Stack ❶ to show only the Main Track, it will display any Automation curves ❷ that exist in any of the Subtracks ❸ as dimmed lines.

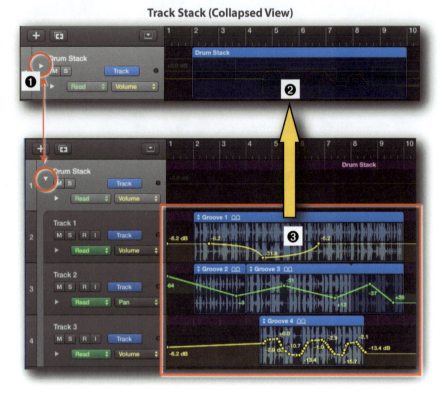

Track Stack (Collapsed View)

Option to Delete Empty Tracks Containing Automation Data

The command *Track ➤ Delete Unused Tracks* ❹ now has an additional option:

- ▶ **10.2.0**: Any Track that didn't contain Regions was deleted
- ▶ **10.2.1**: Any Track that doesn't contain Regions will be deleted, but if such a Track has existing automation data, then a Dialog Window ❺ pops up giving you two options:
  - Delete: Delete the Track with the automation data
  - Cancel: Don't delete the Track with the automation data

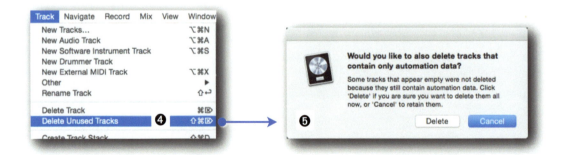

Folder Stack

First Folder Stack named "Sub 1"

Creating your First Folder Stack in your Project will name the Master Track correctly "Sub 1"❶, instead of "Sub 2" as it did in 10.2.

Remember

The Main Track of a Folder Stack is a VCA Channel Strip ❷ named, in this case, "Sub 1". Having the "VCA" Channel Strip Component (VCA Slot ❸) visible, displays the name of the VCA Channel Strip (the VCA Group).

Create and Flatten Track Stacks Command in the Mixer

Mixer Window

The Local Option Menu in the Mixer Window has two new commands ❸:

▶ **Create Track Stack for Selected Channel Strip**
▶ **Flatten Stack**

Record to all Subtracks of a Summing Stack

A Summing Stack not only has advantages when you are mixing, but it now also has a useful functionality for recording:

▶ If the Subtracks of a Summing Stack are Audio Tracks ❹, then record-enabling the Main Track ❺ will automatically record-enable all the included Subtracks ❻.

▶ Make sure that the Audio Channels Strips are set to discrete input channels of your Audio Interface.

Default Selection for unavailable Audio Device

If the currently selected audio device isn't available, Logic now uses one of the other three most recently used audio devices in order of last used (instead of defaulting to the built-in audio hardware).

New "Multithreading" Preference Setting

There is a new Multithreading ❶ setting in the *Preferences ➤ Audio ➤ Devices* tab. Like most of the settings on this page, it requires a deeper understanding on how digital audio is processed on a computer in general, and Logic in particular.

Here is a quick summary about the underlying technology to better understand what this new setting does:

🌑 Technical Background

- ▶ **CPU**: The processing of your digital audio signal is handled by the computer's CPU (central processor unit).

- ▶ **Core**: Modern CPUs have multiple "Cores", which are like multiple CPUs on a single chip. Each Core can handle its own tasks (i.e. processing audio) independently from each other at the same time. Today's computers have CPUs with usually 4 (quad-core), 8, or 12 Cores.

- ▶ **Thread**: Think of a Thread as a series of tasks, a stream of instructions (calculations) that are performed on an individual Core (one Core = one Thread).

- ▶ **Hyper-thread**: A technology called "Hyper-threading" (developed by Intel) lets a single Core perform two calculations (streams of instructions) simultaneously (two Threads parallel). This way, a 4-core processor can function as a virtual 8-core, providing 8 individual Threads per clock cycle.

- ▶ **Multithreading**: Any app (like Logic) has to be programmed to take advantage of those multiple Threads to spread their workload across the individual Threads. There are numerous factors that influence how the OS or an app distributes the workload at any time, which makes it a bit difficult to predict exactly what gets processed on which Thread.

🌑 Logic's Multithreading

Here is how those Cores and Threads relate to Logic:

There is a "*Processing Threads*" ❷ setting in Logic's *Preferences ➤ Audio ➤ Devices* tab. Its popup menu displays the maximum number of Threads ❸ available on your computer. Most Apple computers use Hyper-threading, so the maximum number you see in this menu, divided by two, is the number of Cores available on your computer (listed in your Hardware Settings ❹).

The default setting in Logic is "Automatic" ❸ where Logic decides how many Threads it uses. To monitor the activity of the individual Threads, select the Custom Control Bar Display and *double-click* on the CPU Meter ❺, which opens the standalone Load Meters window ❻. Each vertical bar ❼ on the left represents one Thread indicating its activity (the load). The number of bars reflects the setting in the Processing Threads menu.

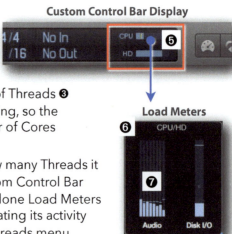

1 Channel Strip = 1 Thread

There is one important fact (limitation) in Logic when it comes to Threads:

> **The Audio Processing on a single Channel Strip can not be distributed to multiple Threads**

All the calculations needed to process the audio signal running through a single Channel Strip (going through all the loaded Plugins on that Channel Strip) has to be performed on one Thread and cannot be spread over multiple Threads. Of course, if you have more Channel Strips than Cores, then multiple Channel Strips are assigned to the available Threads, which one depends on how efficient Logic distributes the load.

➡ *Two Thread Distribution Modes*

Logic uses two different modes when it comes to distributing the audio processing on Channel Strips to the available Threads:

 Playback Mode

This is the default mode where Logic tries to spread the load of each Channel Strip across the available Threads. If you have "too much going on" on a single Channel Strip (too many CPU-intensive Plugins), then you might overload a single Thread (error message!), especially if Logic assigns other Channel Strips to that same Thread too.

Please note that this is not necessarily a Logic limitation and more of a technical challenge. A Plugin acts as one unit and its processing can't be split up by the application to be processed on multiple threads. To do so, the Plugin itself has to be specially coded to divide its workload to multiple Threads (maybe something for the future). For now, all the Plugins on a single Channel Strip act as the main audio processing thread that has to be processed in series on a single Thread.

Your only option for a "fully loaded Channel Strip" is to split the audio signal (and load) to an Aux Channel Strip, which, as a separate Channel Strip, can be handled by a separate Thread.

In general, whenever an audio signal can be rendered in parallel, Logic will use multiple Threads. For example:

- ▶ Multiple Audio Channel Strips.
- ▶ Multiple Instrument Channel Strips, even on a Summing Stack.
- ▶ Channel Strips sending their signals via the Sends to one or more Aux Channel Strips.
- ▶ Multi-Output Software Instrument (MOSI) using separate Aux Channel Strips for the individual outputs.

 Live Input Mode

The Live Input Mode is some mysterious Logic "thing" that makes the already complex subject of Thread-distribution even more, let's say, "interesting". However it is very important, especially when trying to understand the new "Multithreading" settings in LPX 10.2.1.

When selecting a Software Instrument Channel Strip or selecting its Record Enable Button, Logic enters "Live Input Mode" when you start playback or play that Track via MIDI. This takes about 100ms to engage. You might have noticed sometimes when playing your first note on your MIDI Keyboard that the newly selected Track has a little delay on that first note. This is the Live Input Mode kicking in. Live Input Mode will also be enabled on an Audio Channel Strip, not when it is selected, but when it is record-enabled.

The Live Input Mode has a major implication about how Logic distributes the signal processing across multiple Threads. Now all the Channel Strips that are part of the signal flow related to that selected Channel Strip are handled by a single Thread. This is done to ensure low latency during recording (remember, you selected the Track, so Logic assumes that you want to record on it). The major downside, as many Logic users will know, is the higher risk of a system overload message. If you think about it, if an Instrument Channel Strip has a CPU-intensive Instrument Plugin, plus lots of CPU-intensive Audio FX Plugins, routed to multiple Aux Channel Strips (with their own Plugins), and all that routed to the Output Channel Strip with even more Plugins, then all those Channel Strips are processed on a single Thread … Boooom.

Example

Here is an example of a simple Project to show the difference between Playback Mode and Live Input Mode:

I have one Audio Channel Strip ❶ with no Audio Regions playing and next to it are two Instrument Channel Strips ❷ ❸ with the CPU-intensive Alchemy Plugin. The second Instrument uses a send to an Aux Channel Strip that has a couple of Audio FX Plugins loaded ❹. And finally, the Output Channel Strip, also loaded with a few Audio FX Plugins ❺. The screenshot of the Load Meters Window to the left indicates what happens (*double-click* on the CPU Meter in the Custom Control Bar Display to open that window).

🔘 Playback Mode

No Instrument Channel Strip is selected

On the Load Meters ❻, the first two bars (threads) show the CPU activity of the two Instrument Channel Strips. The little bar next to it is the Aux Channel Strip and the last bar represents the Output Channel Strip. Everything is well balanced, no problem.

🔘 Live Input Mode

One Instrument Channel Strip is selected

Life Input Mode

Here is what happens when I select the second Instrument Channel Strip ❼. It switches that Channel Strip to Live Input Mode, which means, this Instrument Channel Strip ❸, plus the Aux Channel Strip ❹, plus the Output Channel Strip ❺ are all processed on a single Thread (the last bar ❽), which now reaches its maximum and might result in an overload message.

The first bar ❾ (Thread) still represents the first Instrument Channel Strip ❷ that is not in Live Input Mode.

Tip: To avoid this situation and the negative "side effect" of Live Input Mode, never leave an Instrument Channel Strip selected if you don't want to record on it. Select an Audio Channel Strip instead, or even better, a Track with No Output ❿ assignment.

Now, after this extended introduction, and hopefully with a better understanding of threading, let's look at that new "Multithreading" settings in LPX 10.2.1 to find out what it does.

➡ Playback & Live Tracks

Live Input Mode can become a huge problem when using Summing Stacks. Let's see what it means in the context of threading.

Summing Stack

Here is an example:

- Remember, the Main Track ❶ of a Summing Stack represents an Aux Channel Strip.
- All the Subtracks ❷ of a Summing Stack represent individual Channel Strips and their outputs are routed to the Main Track's Aux Channel Strip.
- If you use Instrument Channel Strips as the Subtracks, then you can use the Summing Stack to create layered synth sounds.

💀 #1 Main Track not selected

When you play back the Project and the Main Track is not selected, then Logic will distribute the individual Channel Strips of the Subtracks to separate Threads.

▶ Load Meter: The Main Track ❶ and the individual Subtracks ❷ are distributed across the available Threads creating a nice load balance, 5 Channel Strips, 5 Threads ❸.

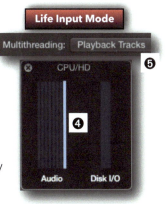

💀 #2 Main Track Selected Multithreading: Playback Tracks

One advantage of the Summing Stack is that you can select the Main Track, and then whatever you play on your external MIDI Controller will be sent to all the Subtracks (all those Instrument Plugins), letting you play that layered sound live. However, this has a bad side effect:

Although the selected Main Track ❶ is an Aux Track, selecting it enables the Live Input Mode on the Summing Stack. Now the entire Summing Stack is treated as one "signal flow" unit, which means, all the 5 involved Channel Strips are processed by a single Thread ❹. This is the behavior when "Playback Tracks" ❺ is selected in the new Multithreading setting (the default behavior in LPX 10.2).

▶ Load Meter: All the Channel Strips of the Summing Stack are processed by one single Thread ❹, which easily can result in a "System Overload" message.

💀 #3 Main Track Selected Multithreading: Playback & Live Tracks

Now, when you select the "Playback & Live Tracks" ❻ option from the Multithreading setting, the individual Channel Strips of the Summing Stack are distributed to individual Threads ❼.

▶ Load Meter: The Threads are again nicely load-balanced. This applies to Logic Instrument Plugins, but also to third-party Instrument Plugins.

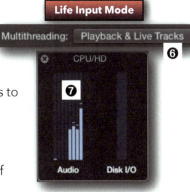

This new "Playback & Live Tracks" setting will also improve the load balance if you record with a high number of Audio Tracks on individual input channels, because Live Input Mode also affects the Audio Channels, which benefit from a more efficient load-balancing across the available Threads.

Force Touch and 3-D Touch Support for Software Instruments

The drum kits and software instruments in Logic now respond to Force Touch and 3-D touch with supported devices.

Move Plugin Window by dragging top or bottom

In addition to moving the Plugin Window by dragging the window header ❶, now you can also drag the lower edge ❷ of the window.

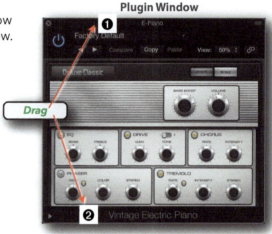

Plugin Window

Sh+click on EQ Thumbnail to Add "Linear Phase EQ"

The EQ Thumbnail area ❸ on the Channel Strip is a very versatile little section:

▸ **Click** on the empty section ❸ to load the Channel EQ Plugin ❹.
▸ _NEW_: **Sh+click** on the empty section to load the Linear Phase EQ Plugin ❺.

Remember

▸ The EQ Thumbnail displays the frequency curve of the Channel Strip EQ ❻ (even animated when automation is used).
▸ The EQ Thumbnail is grayed out when the Plugin is bypassed ❼.
▸ **Click** on the active EQ Thumbnail ❹ (Plugin loaded) to open or close the Channel EQ Plugin Window.
▸ You can **drag** or **opt+drag** the EQ Thumbnail to a different Channel Strip to move it or copy it.

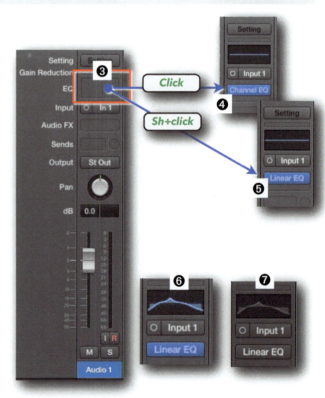

Short Names used on Sends Buttons

To understand the following "improvement" in LPX 10.2.1, you have to be familiar with the I/O Labels Window (Main Menu: **Mix ➤ I/O Labels...**). In this window, you can select the labeling of the three types of busses: "Input Busses", "Output Busses", and "Auxiliary Busses". Please note that Logic uses the term "Bus" instead of the proper term Auxiliary Bus (which is different from the Aux Channel Strip).

You use the radio buttons in this window to determine if you want to use the default name ❶ (Channel column), the name provided by the Driver ❷, or your own User name ❸. You can even enter a Long Name and a Short Name ❹.

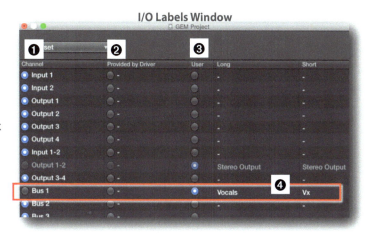
I/O Labels Window

LPX 10.2.1 not only fixes the buggy behavior when entering your custom names (now it's the standard *double-click*, enter name, and hit return), it also changes the behavior about the Auxiliary Busses regarding what name is displayed where.

Here is an example that demonstrates the behavior:

In the I/O Label Window, I selected the radio button for User for Bus 1 ❹ and entered "*Vocals*" as the Long name and "*Vx*" as the Short Name. That means, those names are used in various places instead of the generic label "Bus 1".

Please pay attention to the double button in the upper-right corner of the Mixer Window ❺. It switches between Narrow Channel Strips ▥ ▥ and Wide Channel Strips ▥ ▥. This has an effect on the displayed labels.

▶ **Sends Button**: On a narrow Channel Strip, the Sends Button displays the Short Name ❻ and on a wide Channel Strip, it displays the Long Name ❼, unless it is too long, then it also displays the Short Name.

▶ **Input Button**: If you select a Bus as the Input source for an Aux Channel Strip or Audio Channel Strip, then the display is similar. On a narrow Channel Strip, the Input Button displays the Short Name ❽ and on a wide Channel Strip, it displays the Long Name ❾. If the Long Name is too long, then Logic will truncate the name, leaving out some characters.

▶ **Tooltip**: Moving the Cursor Tool over the Sends Button or Input Button will pop up the little Tooltips. It always displays the Long Name ❿, or the name of the Channel Strip that functions as the send destination.

▶ **Sends Menu / Input Menu**: The Menus that list the 64 Busses (*click-hold* on the Sends Button or the Input Button), list the Long Name ⓫ in parentheses. Be careful, if you haven't selected the User Label for a Bus, then the parentheses list the name(s) of the Aux Channel Strips that use that Bus as their input.

Tooltips

Tooltips displays Plugin Name and Preset

Moving the Mouse Cursor over a Plugin Slot ❶ (blue button) will pop up a Tooltips window ❷ displaying the name of the Plugin (the original name, not the custom name) followed by the name of the loaded Plugin Settings (if one is loaded). This is the same name displayed in the Plugin Settings popup menu ❸ of the Plugin Window.

Power Button for Plugins and Sends works in Ad-Hoc Groups

Logic provides four types of grouping features/techniques in the Mixer Window.

- **Aux Groups**
- **Channel Strip Groups**
- **VCA Groups**
- **Ad-hoc Groups**

Each one has its own strength suited for specific mix techniques. The Ad-hoc Group feature is the fastest one. You select multiple Channel Strips (by clicking on them or dragging across), and whatever change you make on one of the selected Channel Strips will apply to all selected Channel Strips. For example, change the position of the Fader, Pan, Sends, Mute, add Plugin, etc.

Two functions that didn't work in the Ad-hoc Group are now possible in LPX 10.2.1

Toggle Sends Button of Ad-hoc Group

▶ **Power Button on a Send Button**: *Clicking* on the Power Button of a Sends Button ❹ toggles the Power Button on ❺/off ❻ for that Sends Slot on all selected Channel Strips.

▶ **Power Button on a Plugin Button**: *Clicking* on the Power Button of a Plugin Button ❼ toggles the Power Button on ❺/off ❾ for that Plugin Slot on all selected Channel Strips.

Toggle Plugin Button of Ad-hoc Group

Preference to Open Plugin Window in "Controls View"

Most Plugin Windows have two different views:

- ▶ **Controls View ❶**: All the controls of a Plugin are displayed on a black window as a long list of controls (slider, buttons, menus) without any graphical elements.
- ▶ **Editor View ❷** (default): All the controls of Plugin are displayed with a more or less elaborate GUI (graphical user interface).

The View popup menu ❸ on the right side of the Plugin Header lets you select the view.

Now in LPX v10.2.1, you have an additional checkbox in the *Preferences ➤ Display ➤ Mixer ➤ Open in controls view"* ❺, that opens a Plugin Window in the Controls View instead of the (default) Editor View.

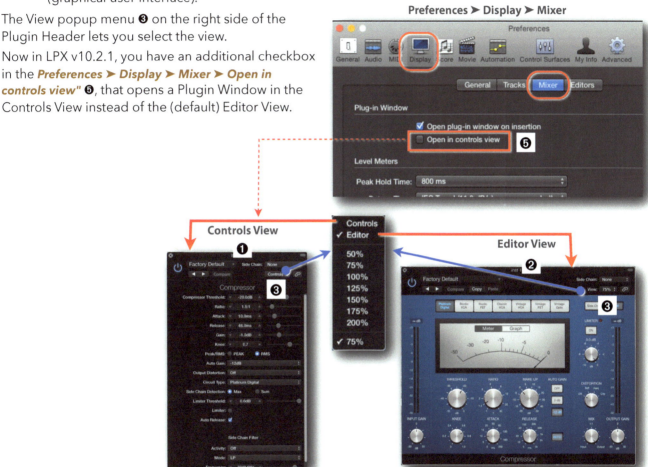

Improved Plugin Delay Compensation (PDC)

Most Plugins introduce latency, a delay between the time the signal "enters" the Plugins and the time it "comes out". This is due to the time the Plugin needs to process the audio signal. Logic can compensate for that Latency during playback by slightly delaying all the signals on your mixer accordingly so they play in sync. This is called **Plugin Delay Compensation**" (PDC) and it can be enabled in the *Preferences ➤ Audio ➤ General ➤ Plug-in Latency*.

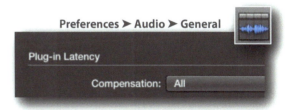

Now in LPX 10.2.1, PDC is also applied to the Playhead and the Meter Displays on the mixer so everything you <u>hear</u> and <u>see</u> is in sync.

New Skin for the Impulse Response Utility

The Impulse Response Utility is a separate application that lets you create (record) your own Impulse Responses. An Impulse Response (IR) is a small audio file (impulse) recorded in an acoustic environment, (i.e. a concert hall) representing the acoustic characteristics of that environment. A so-called "convolution reverb" (like Logic's Space Designer Plugin) can load such an Impulse Response and make any audio signal that you send to the Plugin sound like it is played in that acoustic environment that the specific IR represents (was recorded in).

Logic comes with a wide variety of IRs that are stored in the system Library
/Library /Audio/Impulse Responses/ Apple/. You can also create your own IRs using the Impulse Response Utility.

▶ **Location**: In Logic9, the app was stored as a standalone application in the Utilities folder inside the Applications folder, but now in LPX, it is only available "inside" the Logic Pro X application (when you open Logic with the "Show Package Contents" command
(*Logic Pro X/Contents/Applications/*)

▶ **Launch**: Unless you want to dig into the Logic Package file, you open the Impulse Response Utility from the Space Designer Plugin. *Click* on the tiny triangle ❶ to open a popup menu and select "Open IR Utility…" ❷.

Logic has updated the Impulse Response Utility from 1.0.5 ❸ to 1.0.6 ❹ with a new skin (light gray instead of dark gray). The functionality is the same.

Space Designer

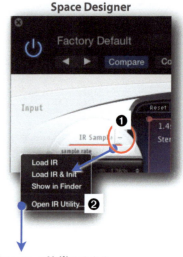

Impulse Response Utility 1.0.5

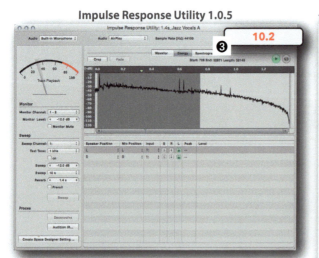

Impulse Response Utility 1.0.6

Read up on the User Guide to learn how to use the app.
https://itunes.apple.com/us/book/logic-pro-x-effects/id960808317?mt=11

Alchemy Improvements

Besides many bug fixes, Alchemy has a lot of improvements in this LPX 10.2.1 update. Here are just a few:

11 New Spectral Effects ❶

New X-button ❷ in the Browser Search Field

Click on the X-button to clear the search field.

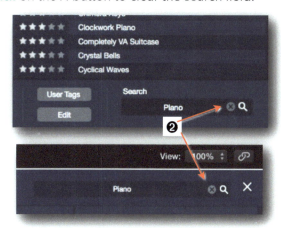

Preset Ratings

Drag left across the stars to remove ❸ the yellow Preset Ratings.

The Default Star Ratings are now light gray ❹ instead of blue.

Label Changes

The Label "Wheel" in the Performance section has been renamed to "ModWheel" ❺.

The label "Sustain" in the Sequencer section has been renamed to "Gate" ❻.

And much, much more:

▶ Alchemy now uses less CPU processing for each instance.

▶ You can drag Apple Loops into Alchemy and they automatically conform to the current tempo.

▶ When you import an Apple Loop into an Alchemy source, settings are automatically configured so the loop can be triggered from any key and play at the current project tempo.

▶ The accuracy of the Detect Tempo options has been significantly improved, especially with long audio files.

▶ Alchemy now supports MIDI mono mode. This lets you use third-party Expressive MIDI Controllers, including products from Roli and Roger Linn Design.

▶ Alchemy now automatically adjusts the gain when morphing formants.

▶ Selecting a filter type in Alchemy now automatically enables the filter.

▶ In Alchemy, the Num-Osc control in Additive synthesis mode has been renamed to Partials to more accurately represent its function.

One way to add an audio sample to the cell of the Drum Machine Designer is to select the cell, open the Library Browser and double-click on an audio sample. Another way is to drag an audio file directly from the Finder onto a cell. But this had a limitation in LPX 10.2.

🟤 LPX 10.2

You can only drag one audio file at a time to the Drum Machine Designer. When you select multiple audio files in the Finder ❶ and drag them onto a cell in the Drum Machine Designer, it looks like you are adding all those files ❷. However, only the first audio file is added to the one cell ❸ you are dragging over.

🟤 LPX 10.2.1

Now when you drag those multiple selected audio files ❹ onto a cell ❺ in the Drum Machine Designer, all those audio files are added to the Drum Machine Designer, populating all the different cells ❻.

- The samples are placed starting on the cell you are placing the cursor, moving to the right and then to the next upper row, and then to the second page.

- Cells with existing audio files are overwritten with the new ones.

- An Alert Window "Not all samples assigned" ❼ pops up if you drag more audio files than there are cells available.

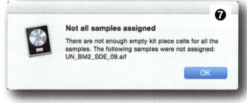

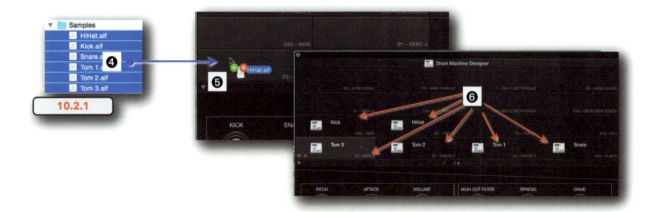

"Empty Kit" Patch for Drum Machine Designer

Loading the Drum Machine Designer (DMD) onto a Track, automatically loads the "Big Room" Patch with one of those complex Summing Stacks configuration that makes up the Drum Machine Designer. This is great if you don't want to mess with the sounds and configuration. However, if you want to tweak a DMD Patch, load your own sounds, or start from scratch, you had to edit an existing Patch.

Library Browser

Now, LPX 10.2.1 has an additional Patch named "Empty Kit" ❶ in the Library Browser, listed with all the other DMD Patches ❷.

This "Empty Kit" Patch loads a simple Summing Stack, only with the Main Stack Channel Strip that has some Audio FX ❸ pre-loaded and the Instrument Channel Strip that has the Ultrabeat Plugin ❹ loaded but without any sounds on it.

"Auto-select" Button in the Drummer Editor

The Drummer Editor can only show one Drummer Region at a time. This is the currently selected Region in the Tracks Window.

Drummer Editor

Now in LPX 10.2.1, the Drummer Editor has a new *Auto-select* Button ❺ in the Region Header that you can toggle on and off by clicking on it. It functions similar to the Catch Playhead (Catch Content). If enabled, the Drummer Editor automatically displays the next Drummer Region if the Playhead in the Tracks Window moves over it.

New Layout and Enhancements for Plugins

Many of the Audio FX Plugins are updated to a new layout and some of them have added functionality. See the separate chapter (Plugin Makeover) for details.

Rename Plugins: Long Names and Short Names

Similar to the I/O Labels window where you can enter custom names for your Input Channels, Output Channels, and Auxiliary Busses, the Plug-In Manager (Main Menu: *Logic Pro X ➤ Preferences ➤ Plug-In Manager*) now lets you also enter your own custom names for all the Plugins. The list pane in the Plug-In Manager has two new columns, "Custom Name" ❶ and "Short Name" ❷. *Double-click* on the field, enter the name, and hit *return*.

▸ **Custom Name**: The Custom Name will be displayed in the Plugin Menu ❸ and also on the bottom of the Plugin window ❹.

▸ **Short Name**: The Short Name will be displayed on the Plugin Button ❺ on the Channel Strip (in wide and narrow view ▦ ▢).

▸ **Name**: Moving the mouse cursor over the Plugin Button will show the Tooltip that still displays the original Plugin name ❻.

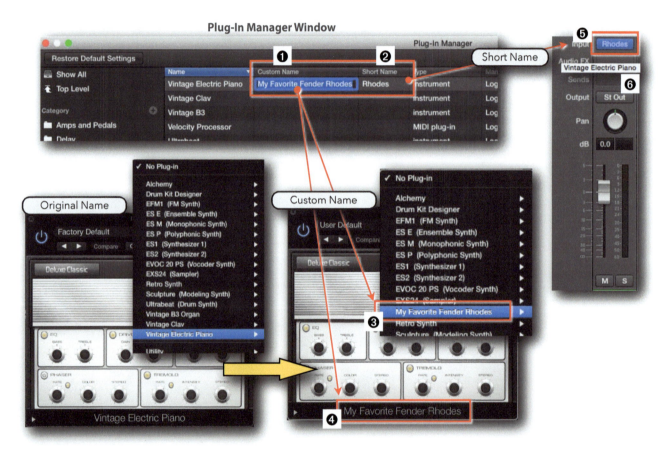

Sort Category Folders in Plugin Manager

The Category Folders ❼ on the left side of the Plug-In Manager window in LPX 10.2 were sorted alphabetically. Now you can arrange them freely by dragging the folders up or down. A blue insertion line ❽ indicates the new position after releasing the mouse.

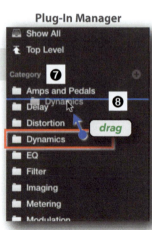

Automatically create new Category Folders in the Plug-In Manager

Usually, you create a new Category Folder in the Plug-In Manager by clicking on the Plus Button ❶ ⊕. Now in LPX 10.2.1, there is another way to do that:

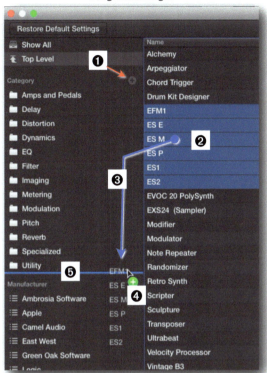

- ☑ Select a group of Plugins in the list ❷.
- ☑ *Drag* those Plugins to the Sidebar on the left ❸.
- ☑ A Plus sign ⊕ appears next to the Pointer Tool and the Plugin Names appear as "ghost names" ❹.
- ☑ When you position the Pointer Tool just below the last Category Folder, a blue insertion line ❺ appears.
- ☑ When you release the mouse, a new Category Folder is created with the name "Untitled" that includes all the Plugins ❷ that you just dragged over.
- ☑ At that moment, the new Category Folder is still highlighted (key focus), so you can enter a name for it right away.
- ☑ Now you can drag that new folder to any position in the Category section.

Bounce Window displays Start-End based on Project Type

The Bounce Window (**cmd+B**) has two entry fields that display the range of your Project that you are about to bounce. It lists the Start time ❶ and the End time ❷ along your Project's timeline. The selection is based on Logic's priority for the bounce selection (active Cycle, selected Regions, or entire Project). So far, the field always displayed the Musical Time in bars:beats. Now in 10.2.1, the displayed unit depends on the current Project Types settings:

Use Musical Grid ❸: The fields display Musical Time in bars:beats ❹

Use Musical Grid ❺: The fields display Absolute Time in SMPTE ❻

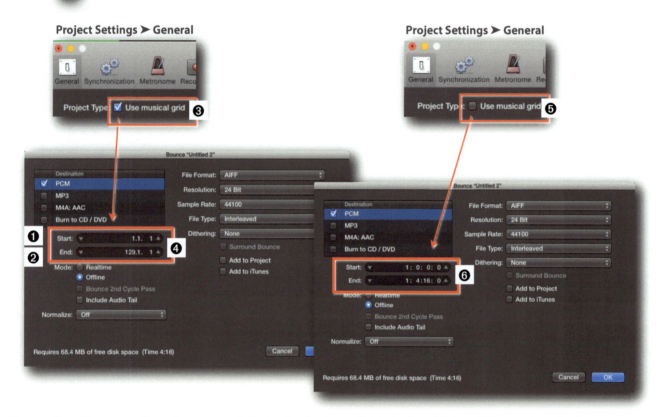

Remember: You can adjust the Start and End value in those fields before hitting OK to initiate the bounce.

Bounce Tracks-in-Place for multiple selected Tracks and Summing Stacks

The command *File ➤ Bounce ➤ Tracks in Place* (Key Command *ctr+cmd+B*) has been extended. Now you can:

▶ Bounce multiple selected Tracks.

▶ Bounce a Summing Stack to bounce the entire stack to a new Track. You can't select the option "Destination: Replace Track".

▶ Bounce any combination of the two.

Export multiple Audio Files, multiple Tracks

LPX 10.2.1 now lets you export multiple selected Tracks or multiple selected Regions as Audio Files.

The Main Menu *File ➤ Export ➤* indicates how many Regions ❶ or how many Tracks ❷ are currently selected.

File ➤ Export ➤

Export Tracks with additional "Limit Export to Cycle Range" Checkbox

The Export Tracks as Audio Files Dialog has an additional checkbox, "*Limit Export to Cycle Range*" ❸, to export the selected Track(s) only between the Cycle Range instead of the entire Project (from the beginning of Project to the end of the last Region on that Track).

Project Browser vs. Audio Bin

The Export Track Dialog also has a little cosmetic change. Although Logic Pro X renamed the "Audio Bin" to "Project Audio", this window still used the old terminology for the checkbox "Add resulting files to Audio Bin" ❹. Now in 10.2.1, it finally has been updated to "Add resulting files to Project Audio" ❺.

Export Track Dialog

Attention

Please note that using the "Limit Export to Cycle Range" has a potential bug regarding the timestamp.

When Logic creates a new audio file (recording, bouncing, export), it adds various Metadata (data about data) to that file. One of those Metadata is a so-called timestamp, information when the recording of that Audio File started in your Project (i.e. 1h12m30s00f). When you import that audio file later into another Project, you can use Logic's "**Move to Original Recording Position**" to place it at the exact time position where it was recorded. Of course, you can also use that command after you moved a Region around (or when importing the file to another DAW like Pro Tools).

When using the new "Limit Export to Cycle Range" feature, Logic uses the time position of the Project Start as the timestamp and not the time position of the left locator of the Cycle Range as you would expect.

New "Sound Library" item in the Logic Pro X Menu

LPX 10.2 only had the menu item "Download Additional Content..." ❶ in the Logic Pro X Main Menu. Now in LPX 10.2.1, there is a new submenu "**Sound Library**" ❷ that contains a total of four menu items ❸ for better management of the Logic Content:

▶ **Download Essential Sounds**

▶ **Download All Available Sounds**

▶ **Reinstall Sound Library**

▶ **Open Sound Library Manager...**

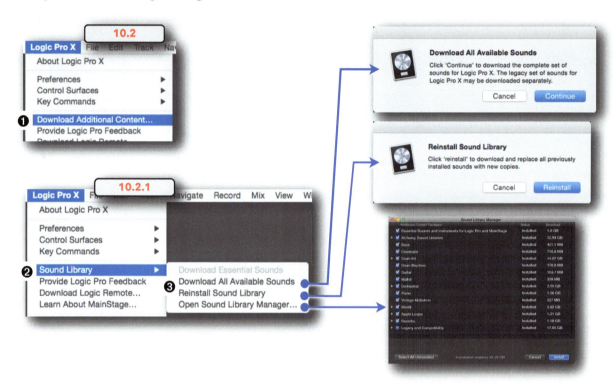

BTW, you no longer have to download the Essential Sounds Library before you can open Logic.

New Download Glyph

The Loop Browser and the Library Browser now show a new Download Glyph ❹ 🔽 if a specific file (or category) is not downloaded yet (the name is grayed out).

Clicking on that glyph will start the download. During the download, the grayed out files (and category folders) will display a circular progress indicator ❺.

Additional Dialog Windows for Download Manager

In addition to the new Sound Library Menu Commands, LPX v10.2.1 provides much better Dialog Windows and procedures to manage (or interrupt) download processes of Logic Content.

Control Bar Display

▶ Any download process is indicated by a progress bar ❶ that is displayed under the Display Mode Button in the LCD.

▶ *Click* on the Progress Bar to open a Popover Window ❷ listing the individual tasks. This functions as a Task Manager.

▶ When a content download is in progress, the Popover displays the following information:

- Progress Bar
- Name of the download
- Size of the file
- Size of the download so far
- Remaining *time* to completion, *idle* (waiting in line), or *stopped* (paused download)
- **Pause Button** ❸ : You can pause any download process, in case you currently need the bandwidth for something else.
- **Resume Button** ❹ : The Pause Button changes to a Resume Button when pressed, that lets you continue with the download.
- **Cancel Button** ❺ : If you click the button, an additional Dialog Window pops up to confirm that action ❻.

▶ Once the download is completed, you will be prompted with an additional Dialog ❼ to enter your Username and Password. Please note that the download process is only step one, where the downloaded installer file is stored on your drive. Once completed, the actual installation process starts (step two), which requires authentication if the installer file stores individual sound files inside your System Library.

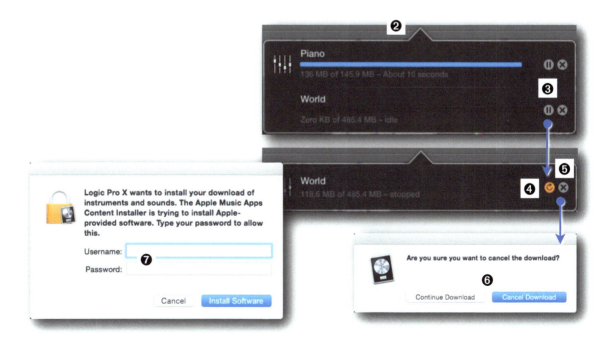

Long Channel Strip Names in the Environment

The display of the Channel Strip Names in the Environment Window has changed for the better:

▶ **10.2**: The Channel Strips could only display a single line for the Channel Strip Name and if the name is pretty long, then it extended to the left and right of the Channel Strip ❶. This was not a problem if you look at one Channel Strip, but if multiple Channel Strips were placed next to each other (as usual), then you could end up with an un-readable mess ❷.

▶ **10.2.1**: Now the Channel Strip Name doesn't extend beyond the left and right border of the Channel Strip, but wraps to up to five lines ❸. Any text that is longer will be truncated and indicated by an ellipses (…)
This provides a much better view when looking at multiple Channel Strips with longer Channel Strip Names ❹.

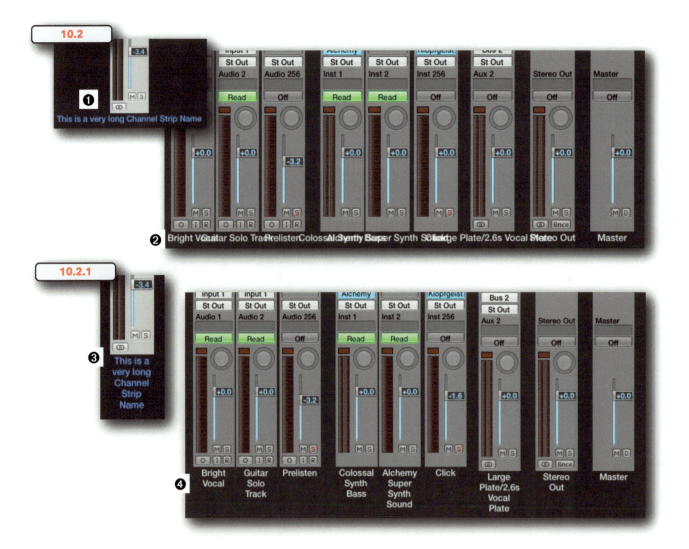

Connected Devices in AMS are shown as Port Names

The Audio MIDI Setup (AMS) utility, located in */Applications/Utilities/*, lets you manage the MIDI Devices that OSX recognizes, and therefore, are available to Logic. Its MIDI Studio Window ❶ displays the three default Devices ❷ "IAC Driver", "Network", and "Bluetooth", plus any external MIDI Devices that are connected to your computer and recognized by OSX. In this screenshot, that would be the Master Keyboard ❸ and a MIDI Interface ❹ (iConnect).

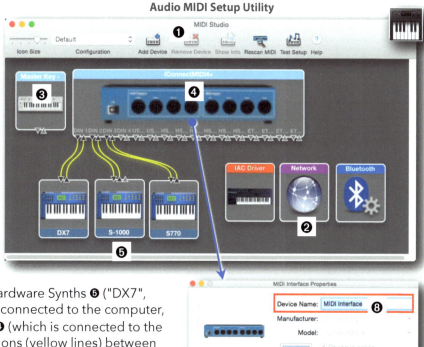

Audio MIDI Setup Utility

In addition, I also created three MIDI Devices in the MIDI Studio Window manually. These are three Hardware Synths ❺ ("DX7", "S1000", "S770") that are not directly connected to the computer, but connected to the MIDI Interface ❹ (which is connected to the computer). I drew the virtual connections (yellow lines) between the Synth and the MIDI Interface to show which MIDI Ports on the interface they are connected to.

However, there was a problem with how the Physical Input Object in the Clicks & Ports Layer of the Environment Window showed those Devices.

10.2: The Physical Input Object shows only the devices that represent (are connected to) a specific port on the computer, for example, USB, IAC, Bluetooth, or Network. The manually created Devices in the AMS ❺ will not be displayed, only the actually Devices (and their ports) that are connected to the computer ❻.

Also, the custom Device Names you give some MIDI Devices are not properly displayed.

10.2.1: You can see on the screenshot that, instead of displaying the port names of the Audio Interface DIN 1, DIN 2, and DIN 3, the Physical Input Object displays the names of the manually created Devices that are connected to those ports ❼ ("DX7", "S1000", "S770").

Also, the Physical Input Object can display the custom Display Name you entered in the AMS. For example, I used "MIDI Interface" ❽ and Master Key ❾. Even the Session Names for the Network Device are now displayed properly ❿.

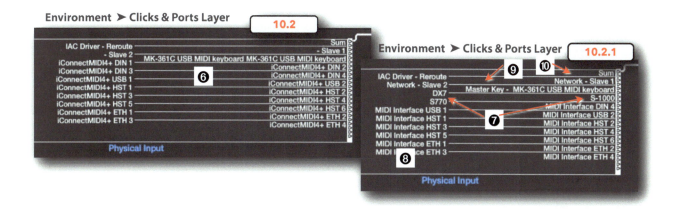

External Controller

Connect Multiple iPads and iPhones running Logic Remote

10.2: In LPX 10.2, when you try to connect a second iPad running Logic Remote, you get an Error Message ❶, warning that Logic will replace the previously connected iPad.

10.2.1: Now, in 10.2.1 you can have multiple iPads and iPhones running Logic Remote connected to Logic. Yes the Logic Remote app for iOS was also updated and can now run on an iPhone (yippie!).

A few quick notes:

▶ All the connected iOS devices, running Logic Remote, will show up in the Control Surface Setup window ❷. Main Menu *Logic Pro X ➤ Control Surfaces ➤ Setup...*

▶ It looks like you can create Control Surface Groups to create one big virtual unit out of multiple iOS Devices (check the Control Surface Bars ❸). I didn't have time to fully test that yet.

▶ The iPhone version of Logic Remote provides a simplified version. In portrait mode ❹, you have two Channel Strips with a few controls, and turning it to landscape mode ❺ switches to the Key Commands View.

iPhone (Logic Remote)

Control Surface Setup Window

Check out my manual "[Logic Remote - How it Works](#)" for more information on that app.

More Reliable Logic Remote Connectivity

Many Logic users have issues with proper connectivity between the Logic Remote and the Logic Pro. Hopefully, that will improve based on the following note in the official Release Notes:

"Logic now connects reliably to Logic Remote in cases where your computer has two IP addresses on the same network (such as when it's connected to both Wi-Fi and Ethernet)"

Apple Remote Control Works Again

You can now control Logic using the Apple Remote Control again, if you still have one lying around.

Apple Remote is a little remote control that came with the old AppleTV. It uses an IR signal (infrared) and can be used on any Mac that has a built-in IR receiver.

Check in your System Profiler under USB ❶ if your Mac has an IR Receiver and make sure that it is not disabled in the ***System Preferences ➤ Security & Privacy ➤ General ➤ Advanced*** ❷ (or just point the thing at your Mac and see if Logic is responding).

System Profiler

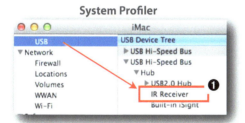

System Preferences ➤ Security & Privacy

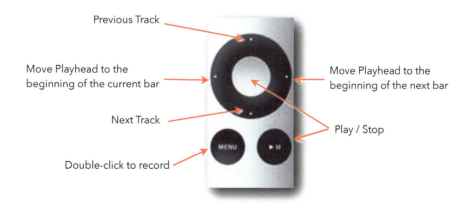

Previous Track

Move Playhead to the beginning of the current bar

Move Playhead to the beginning of the next bar

Next Track

Play / Stop

Double-click to record

New Key Equivalent for the "Floating" Tool Menu

Logic has a Key Command named "Show Tool Menu" that is assigned to the key **T**. This pops up a Tool Menu at the cursor position. This is a special Tool Menu that I like to call "Floating Tool Menu". It has Key Equivalents ❶ assigned to each Tool that act as temporary Key Commands. Key Equivalent that you have assigned in the Key Command Window are ignored as long that Floating Tool Menu is visible. Those Key Equivalents on that Floating Tool Menu have changed:

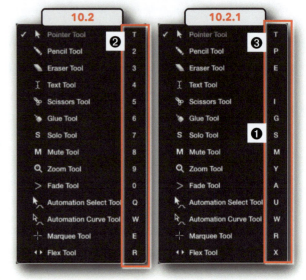

Floating Tool Menu

- ▸ **10.2**: Key Equivalents ❷ were assigned to the Tools on the menu in sequential order from top to bottom, using first the numbers and then the next row of keys on the keyboard (Q, W, E, …). This concept was questionable, because the Floating Tool Menu lists different Tools depending on which window has key focus (Tracks Window, Score, Editor, Audio Track Editor, etc.). However, the key assignment was always strict sequential, resulting in different key assignments for the same Tool in different Floating Tool Menus.

- ▸ **10.2.1**: Now each Tool has a specific fixed Key Equivalent ❸ regardless of which Floating Tool Menu. Most of them use the first letter of the actual Tool. This makes it much easier to remember (Pencil, Glue, Solo, Eraser, etc.).

➡ *The Concept of Tools and Tool Menus*

The implementation of the various Cursor Tools in Logic can be a little bit confusing with all the different ways on how to switch to a specific Tool, manually or automatically. The new "Tool Latch Mode" in 10.2.1 adds to the complexity. To help better understand those concepts, I like to review that topic as a little bonus in this manual.

A Tool is basically the function of the mouse cursor, indicated by its shape. The default function is the Pointer Tool indicated by the arrow ▔. The main concept in Logic, you have to understand first, is that there are three mechanisms that change the Cursor Tool.

💡 **Three Mechanisms**

- ▸ **Main Tool - manually**: This is the main Tool that you choose manually by selecting it from a so-called Tool Menu or with a Key Command. There are different variations that I explain in the next section.
- ▸ **Click Zones - automatically**: This mechanism changes the Tool automatically when you move the mouse over a specific area or object, a so-called Click Zone (i.e. Resize Tool, Loop Tool, etc.). Moving the cursor away switches back to the current Main Tool.
- ▸ **Global Modifier - temporarily**: This mechanism changes the Tool temporarily as long as you hold down a specific modifier key(s). For example, in the Tracks Window, *ctr+opt* for the Zoom Tool 🔍, *sh+ctr* for the Fade Tool, or *ctr+opt* for the Velocity Tool (in the Piano Roll).

👤 Main Tool

The Main Tool, the one you choose manually, has many options and variations which can be potentially confusing. Here are the things you have to be aware of:

▶ **Windows with Switchable Tools**: Only in six windows (Main Window, Piano Roll, Score Editor, Step Editor, Audio Track Editor, Audio File Editor, Environment Window) you can choose a different Main Tool other than the Pointer Tool.

▶ **Tool Menu**: Those Windows (or Window Panes) that let you switch Tools, have a Tool Menu where you can select one of the available Tools. Just *click* on the Tool Menu Button ❶ in the Menu Bar that opens a popup menu with the available Tools to choose from.

▶ **Available Tools**: The Tools Menu in these six windows are different, listing only the Tools that make sense (are needed) in that window.

▶ **Independent Tools**: Each Window or Window Pane remembers the selected Tool for that specific window and the currently selected Tool is also stored with the Screensets.

▶ **3 Tool Menus**: On each window you can (pre-) select up to three different Tools from the Tool Menu Buttons ❷. Those three Tools are assigned to three different click actions:

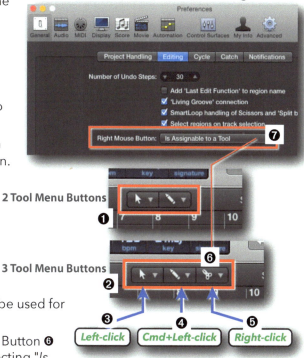

Preferences ➤ General ➤ Editing

  - Left Click Tool ❸: *Clicking* with the left button of the mouse uses that Tool as the click action.

  - Command Left Click Tool ❹: Holding down the command key while *clicking* with the left button of the mouse uses that Tool as the click action.

  - Right Click Tool ❺: *Clicking* with the right button of the mouse uses that Tool as the click action. A *ctr+click* is often used as a substitute for the right click, but cannot be used for this action.

▶ **Show/hide Right Click Tool:** The third Tool Menu Button ❻ is hidden by default and has to be enabled by selecting "*Is Assigned to a Tool*" ❼ from the in the **Preferences ➤ General ➤ Editing**.

👤 Left Click Tool

The selection for the Left Click Tool ❸ is special, because it can be set in different ways:

▶ **Tool Menu Button**: Click on the Tool Menu Button ❷ in the window's Menu Bar and select the Tool from the popup menu.

▶ **Key Command**: The Key Commands Window provides a list of all the Tools, so you can assign a key combination to switch to a specific Tool. Please note that this switches only the Left Click Tool, not the other two (Command Left Click or Right Click). Although the Key Commands are named "Set ...", they are actually "Toggle" commands, toggling between that specific Tool and the Pointer Tool.

▶ **Floating Tool Menu**: This is the special Tool Menu (a Shortcut Menu) that can be easily confused with the Tool Menus (Popup Menus) that open when you click on the corresponding buttons ❷ on the Menu Bar.

▶ **Tool Latch Mode**: This is a new feature in LPX 10.2.1 that temporarily switches the current Left Click Tool to a different Tool based on the key equivalent you press down. Once you click with the mouse, the Tool returns to the previously selected Tool. The Key Equivalent can be a Key Command from the Key Command Window or one of the temporarily Key Equivalents on the Floating Tool Menu. More on that in the next topic.

🌐 Floating Tool Menu

The Floating Tool Menu can be opened in three ways:

▶ ❶ Use the Key Command "Show Tool Menu", which is assigned to *T*. It opens right at your cursor position.

▶ ❷ If you've set the *Preferences ➤ General ➤ Editing ➤ Right Mouse Button* to "Opens Tool Menu", then clicking the right mouse button will open the Floating Tool Menu.

▶ ❸ If you've set the Preferences to "Opens Tool and Shortcut Menu", then clicking the right mouse button will open one long menu with the Floating Tool Menu and the standard Shortcut Menu together.

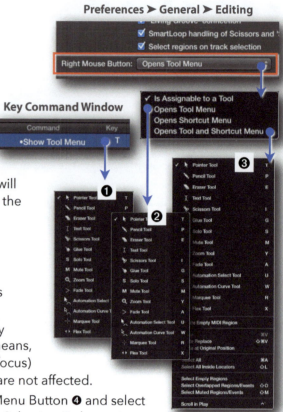

🌐 Left Click Tool - The Whole Picture

Here is a diagram that shows an overview with all the elements involved in setting the Left Click Tool.

▶ Please remember that the following mechanisms apply separately to all the windows with a Tool Menu. That means, it always sets the Left Click Tool ❹ for the current (key focus) window and the Left Click Tool for the other windows are not affected.

▶ **Switch Tool with Menu Selection**: *Click* on the Tool Menu Button ❹ and select the Tool from that Tool Menu ❺. That means, the Menu Selection ❻ determines the Left Click Tool.

▶ **Switch Tool with Key Stroke**: You can set the Left Click Tool with a Key Stroke ❼ using any of the Key Commands ❽ that you can assign to a Tool or use the keys assigned to the Floating Tool Menu ❾ (of course, you can also click on a menu item to select it). The keys of the open Floating Tool Menu have priority over any Key Commands with the same key assignment as long as this menu is open.

▶ **Tool Latch Mode**: Tool Latch Mode ❿ is technically a variation of the Key Stroke switching method. You use the Key Commands ❽ or the assigned Keys from the Floating Tool Menu ❾ to switch the Left Click Tool temporarily only as long as you are pressing down the key.

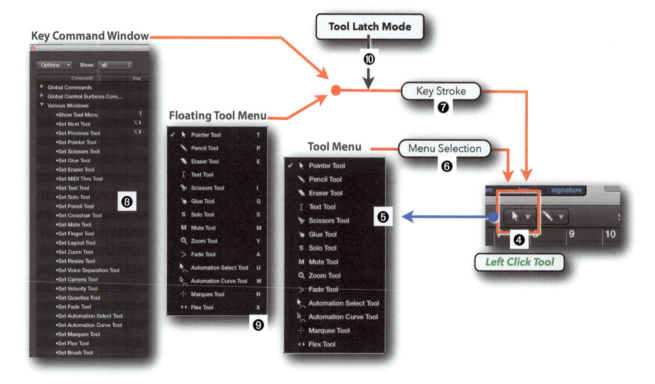

➡ *Floating Tool Menu*

There are a few important things to know about the new Key Equivalents in the Floating Tool Menu in LPX 10.2.1.

▸ The Key Equivalents displayed in the Floating Tool Menu are fixed Key Commands. You cannot re-assign the Tools to different Key Commands.

▸ The Key Equivalent assigned to the Key Command "Show Tool Menu" ❶ will not be available on the menu. As a default, it is assigned to the letter T and that's why the Text Tool has no assignment ❷.

▸ Assigning any other key to the Key Command "Show Tool Menu" (for example, the escape key ❸ 🔄), makes the Text Tool assignment T ❹ visible again.
Please note that the esc key is used system-wide as "Exit Full Screen Mode" and has priority if you are currently in Full Screen Mode.

▸ The Key Equivalent for "Show Tool Menu" ❶ not only opens the Floating Tool Menu, but it is also used as the Key Equivalent for the Pointer Tool ❺ on that Floating Tool Menu. If, at any point, you want to switch to the Pointer Tool, just press that key twice, which represents the following sequence: "Open Floating Tool Menu - Select Pointer Tool - Close Floating Tool Menu".

Here are the screenshots of all the Floating Tool Menus displaying their new Key Equivalents in LPX 10.2.1

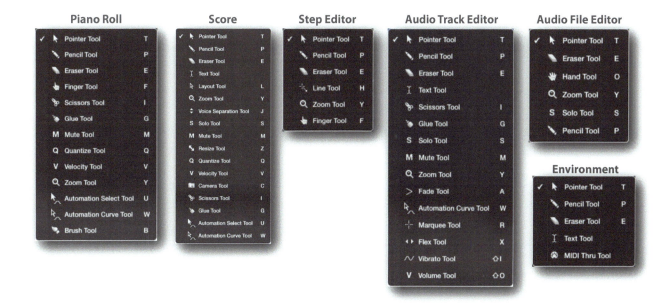

And here is an overview of all the Tools:

▶ ❶ All the Tools that are available on the various Floating Tool Menus

▶ ❷ Key Equivalents assigned to those Tools on the Floating Tool Menu

▶ ❸ Tools available in the Key Commands Window ❺ that can be assigned a Key Equivalent

▶ ❹ Seven columns representing the seven different Floating Tool Menus indicating which Tools are listed on that menu

▶ ❺ This is the list of all Key Commands in the Key Commands Window. Please note that it lists the "Crosshair Tool" ❻, which is the same as the "Line Tool" available in the Step Editor.

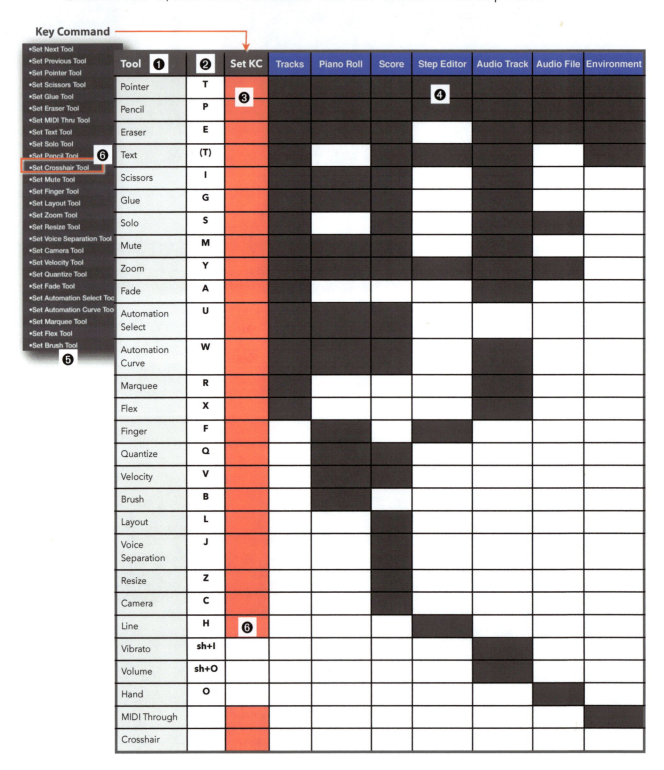

New "Tool Latch Mode" for temporarily switching the Left Click Tool

After that in-depth discussion of the previous topic about the Tools implementation in Logic, let's look at the new feature in LPX 10.2.1, "Tool Latch Mode". It lets you temporarily switch the Left Click Tool with a one-click action.

🔮 Tool Latch Mode

The idea behind that latch procedure is to reduce the additional step of switching back to the previous Tool when you just want to do a quick edit. Here are the two procedures:

▶ **Switch Tool Mode**

When you switch Tools with the Key Command ❶ or the Key Equivalent on the Floating Tool Menu, you use the following three steps:

> ☑ Step 1: Use the Key Command to switch the Left Click Tool to the Tool you need.
> ☑ Step 2: Perform the edit(s) with this Tool.
> ☑ Step 3: Use a Key Command again to switch back to the previous Tool.

▶ **Latch Tool Mode**

With the Latch Tool Mode, you don't need Step 3 of switching back to the previous Tool. Instead of pressing the corresponding key combination, you press and keep holding down the key(s) for a specific Tool for as long as you need it to do the edit(s) with this Tool and then release the key. The Tool automatically switches back to the previous Tool.

Here is an example where the Glue Tool is assigned to the key *W* ❷

> ☑ *Click-hold* the key *W* and the Cursor Tool switches to the Glue Tool (when it is moved over a Region or Event).
> ☑ *Click* to perform the edit action(s) with the Glue Tool and release the *W* key. The Tool automatically switches back to whatever Tool was selected previously.

🔮 Tool Latch Mode with Floating Tool Menu

The Tool Latch Mode also works with the Key Equivalents ❸ in the Floating Tool Menu. However, you have to open the Floating Tool Menu first, using the assign Key Command (i.e. Key *T*) or the other commands I discussed in the previous section. Once open, you can use any of those Key Equivalents to hold down, perform the click edits (at this moment the Floating Tool Menu disappears), and release the key when done with the edit.

Additional "Beat Grouping" option for the Metronome

The *Project Settings* ➤ *Metronome* pane has a new setting called "Group" ❶. Let's review a few things to better understand what that is and how it works:

Global Signature Track

🔘 Time Signature

Logic lets you set the Time Signature(s) of your Project in various places: Control Bar Display, Global Signature Track, Signature List, and even the Score Editor. You set the upper number (Nominator, Number of Beats) and the lower number (Denominator, Beat Value) of a fraction ❷. For example, 5/4.

🔘 Beat Grouping

The upper number of a time signature can be "grouped" (broken up) into two or more numbers, which is referred to as a "Composite Signature" (This was labeled incorrectly "Compound Signature" ⓫ in Logic prior to 10.2.1). For example, the 5 beats in a 5/4 signature is grouped as [3+2]/4 ❸ or [2+2+1]/4 ❹. You can easily set the Beat Grouping in the Time Signature Window ❺ that you open by *double-clicking* on the time signature in the Global Signature Track ❷ or the Score Editor ❻.

🔘 Metronome "Beat Click"

The Beat Grouping has an effect on the Metronome Click "Beat":

<u>No Beat Grouping</u> ❼: The Beat Clicks plays on any beat except the first one (which is the Bar Click) ❽.

<u>Yes Beat Grouping</u> ❸ ❹: The Beat Click plays only on the first beat of every group (except the first one) ❾ ❿.

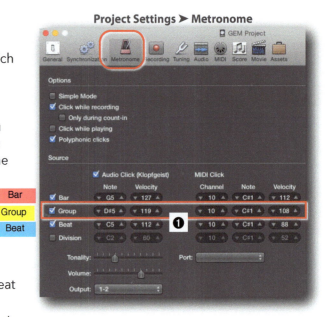

Project Settings ➤ Metronome

🔘 Metronome "Group Click"

This new Group Click plays only when a Beat Grouping is set in the Time Signature Window ❸ ❹. In this case, it plays all the "remaining" Beats that are not played by the Bar Click or Beat Click ❾ ❿.

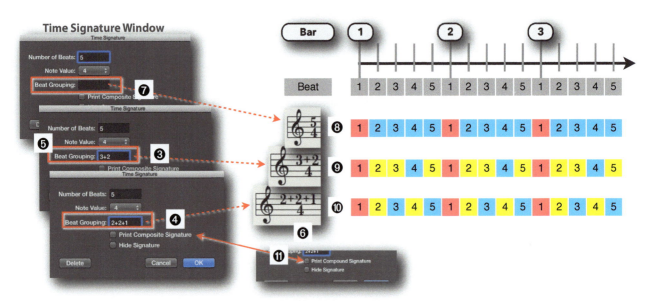

Metronome (Klopfgeist) Sound Settings are stored with the Project

The difference between the Preferences and the Project Settings is that all the configurations in the Project Settings are stored with the Project File (applying only to that Project) and the configurations in the Preferences are stored in the Preferences File, which apply to any Project you open in Logic.

However, there was a strange exception to that rule regarding the sound settings for the Klopfgeist ❶. Although those settings were located in the *Project Settings ➤ Metronome*, they were stored in the Preferences File and not in the Project File. Now in LPX 10.2.1, that has been corrected and those settings are finally stored with the individual Project File.

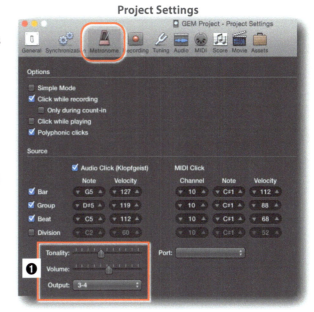

Project Settings

Movie Start Time with negative SMPTE time

You cannot set the "Bar Position plays at SMPTE" time ❷ in the *Project Settings ➤ Synchronization ➤ General* earlier than 0h0m0s0f, but in the *Project Settings ➤ Movie* page, you can now set the Movie Position to a negative SMPTE time ❸.

Please note that the Movie Start time is a relative position to the "plays at SMPTE" time that represents the Absolute Time reference in reference to the Musical Time reference set in the "Bar Position" ❹, which is independent (but most often the same) as the Project Start Position.

Negative Movie Start times might not be needed if you set the Absolute Time reference ❷ to 1h0m0s0f, which is the standard in film music.

Project Settings

New Overlapping Audio Recordings Option in Cycle Mode: "Create Tracks"

There is one additional Overlapping Audio Recording Mode for Cycle and No Cycle recordings. It can be selected in the *Project Settings ➤ Recording ➤ Overlapping Recordings* or the Main Menu *Record ➤ Overlapping Audio Recordings ➤*

▶ No Cycle: **Create New Track ❶**

▶ Cycle: **Create Tracks ❷**

MIDI Clock Delay unit changed from Ticks to ms

The unit for the "*Delay transmission by*" value of the MIDI Clock in the *Project Settings ➤ Synchronizations* pane changed:

▶ **10.2**: Range from -36ticks to 127ticks

▶ **10.2.1**: Range from -200ms to 500ms

Overview

27 of the Audio FX Plugins have been updated in LPX 10.2.1, plus the Klopfgeist Instrument Plugin:

▸ The Plugins now share a new blue UI (User Interface) design that is more "flat".

▸ Some Plugins contain new features or enhancements.

▸ All the Plugins are fully scaleable and ready to be displayed on a hi-resolution Retina display.

Here are all the Audio FX Plugin submenus menus where I added shades to indicate which ones have been updated:

- **Blue Shade**: These are the Plugins that were updated in LPX 10.2.1
- **Gray Shade**: These are Plugins with an individual UI, that might not get updated
- **Black**: These are Plugins that still have the old blue UI and might get updated in the future

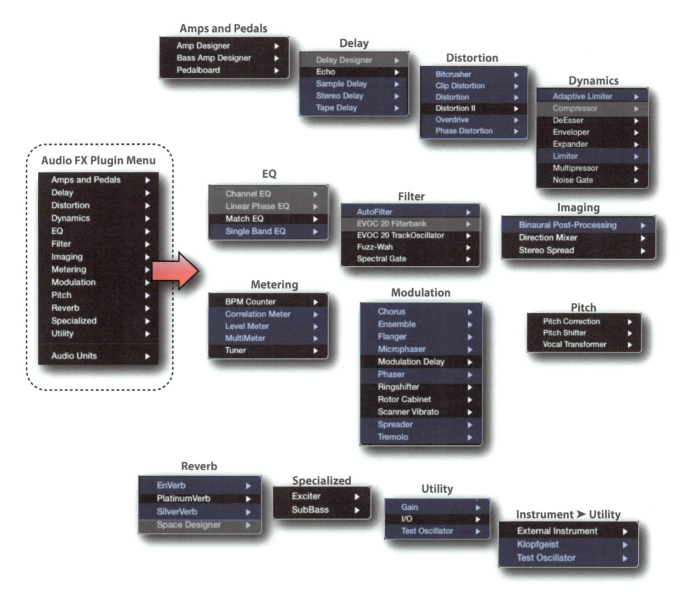

Delay

Sample Delay

Not much has changed in the Sample Delay

▶ **Editor View**: The Plugin now has an Editor View, which it didn't have before.

▶ **Delay Units**: You can switch the delay units between Samples and milliseconds (ms) ❶.

Stereo Delay

The Stereo Delay Plugin has quite a few enhancements:

▸ **Stereo Link**  ❶: This new button links all the controls (not the buttons) of the left and right delay. Changing the value of one control will change the corresponding control relative to each other. Hold the *command* key to temporarily disengage the Stereo Link functionality.

▸ **Routing** ❷: A new popup menu lets you select various presets for the left and right delay routing.

▸ **Tempo Sync** ❸: This button was previously named *Beat Sync*.

▸ **Low Cut / High Cut** ❹: This filter was only available as a global control, but now, each delay has its separate filter.

▸ **Note Value** ❺: Instead of the four note buttons, you now have a popup menu with 14 note values, including dotted and triplet values.

▸ **Delay Time** ❻: The units on the Delay Time knob can change between Absolute Time or Musical Time depending on the Tempo Sync.

▸ **Setting Delay Time**: *Dragging* the knob allows to set values between the note values. *Clicking* on the note labels around the knob snaps to times with deviation set to 0%.

▸ **Double/Half Button** ❼: Two buttons quickly let you change the delay to twice as fast or half as fast.

▸ **Deviation** ❽: This button was previously named *Groove*.

Tape Delay

The Tape Delay has also a couple of changes and enhancements:

- ▶ **Layout**: The different sections of the Plugins are better organized with big labels.
- ▶ **LFO Intensity ❶**: This control was previously named *LFO Depth*.
- ▶ **Clip Threshold ❷**: This control was previously named *Distortion Level*.
- ▶ **Tape Head *Mode* ❸**: This is a new control with two modes, *Clean* and *Diffuse*.
- ▶ **Spread**: This is also a new control to set the stereo width from -100 … +100 ❹.
- ▶ **Feedback**: Not only is the range for the Feedback extended from 100% max to 600% max, the value where the level of the delay increases is now 100% instead of 50%.

The controls in the Delay section are now much easier to setup:

- ▶ **Note ❺**: Instead of just five note values, you have a popup menu with 17 note values. That means, you don't have to combine a note value with a groove percentage anymore to get triplets or dotted notes.
- ▶ **Deviation ❻**: You still can use percentage values (-34% … +50%) to offset the delay value similar to the previous Groove parameter.
- ▶ **Double/Half Button ❼**: You can change the current delay value by clicking on the "x2" button to double it, or clicking on the ": 2" button to set it to half.
- ▶ **Setting Delay Time**: *Dragging* the knob allows you to set values between the note values. *Clicking* on the note labels around the knob snaps to times with deviation set to 0%.

Distortion

Distortion
Bitcrusher   ▶
Clip Distortion   ▶
Distortion   ▶
Distortion II   ▶
Overdrive   ▶
Phase Distortion   ▶

Bitcrusher

Here is what's new:

▶ The Parameters are the same in the new version.

▶ **Modes ❶**: The three Modes now have names: *Fold - Clip - Wrap*.

▶ **Graph ❷**: The graph has a much higher resolution.

▶ **Clip Level**: Now the Clip Level can also be set graphically by dragging the Control Point ❸ of the horizontal line on the graph.

Clip Distortion

Not much changed besides the new layout and graph.

▶ The Parameters are the same in the new version.

▶ The *Tone*, *Clip Filter*, and *Symmetry* parameters can now be edited graphically by dragging the Control Points ❹ in the graph.

Distortion

The four controls are still the same, but the new graphics for the *Drive* and *Tone* Parameter gives you a better picture about what is happening.

Overdrive

Two small changes in the Overdrive Plugin:

▶ **Level Compensation ❶**: The *Level Compensation* on/off parameter that is available in the Distortion Plugin is now also available in the Overdrive Plugin.

▶ **Graph ❷**: The new graph is much more useful, showing the individual curves for *Drive* and *Tone*.

Phase Distortion

All the controls are the same:

▸ **Delay ❸**: The label for *Max Modulation* has been changed to Delay.

▸ **Graph ❹**: The new graph now shows the blue frequency response (controlled by the Cutoff and Resonance control) and the green waveform (controlled by the Intensity control).

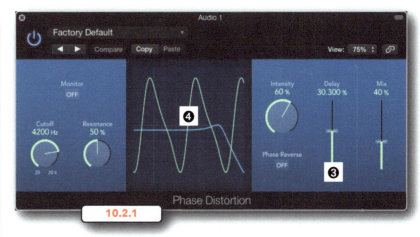

Dynamics

Adaptive Limiter

The Adaptive Limiter has a few minor changes:

> **Reduction Meter**: A separate *Reduction Meter* ❶ displays the real-time gain reduction (from top to bottom) that is applied by the Plugin. This is the same value displayed by the purple Gain Reduction Meter ❷ on the Channel Strip.

> **No more Input Scale**: The *Input Scale* ❸ parameter was removed.

> **Numeric L-R Meter**: The numeric *Peak Meters* ❹ are now displayed for the left and right channels individually.

> **Apply Optimal Lookahead**: The *Optimal Lookahead* value has a new "*Apply*" button ❺. *Clicking* on it will set the Lookahead Knob above to that value.

> **Plugin Delay Compensation (PDC)**: The timing of the Meters is now correct, following the Plugin Delay Compensation.

Limiter

These are the changes for the Limiter:

▶ **Input / Output Meter**: In addition to the *Gain Reduction Meter*, the Plugin also shows the Input and Output Meters ❶ like in the Adaptive Limiter.

▶ **True Peak Detection**: The available parameters are the same. Only the "*Mode*" popup menu has the *Precision ISP* (Inter Sample Peak) item removed ❷. Instead, it is now available as an additional button when the "Precision" ❸ Mode is selected, which changes the "Soft Knee" button ❹ to the "True Peak Detection" button ❺ that you can turn on/off.

▶ **Plugin Delay Compensation (PDC)**: The timing of the Meters is now correct, following the Plugin Delay Compensation.

▶ **Surround**: The Plugin only displays the Reduction Meter ❻ on a Surround Channel Strip and not the Input and Output Level Meters.

Surround

EQ

Single Band EQ

The Single Band EQ Plugin only had the Control View ❶ available showing the four parameters as basic controls. Now the parameters are displayed in the new blue Editor View ❷.

Filter

AutoFilter

Filter

AutoFilter	▶
EVOC 20 Filterbank	▶
EVOC 20 TrackOscillator	▶
Fuzz-Wah	▶
Spectral Gate	▶

There are quite a few changes in the Auto Filter Plugin:

▸ **On/off**: Each section has its individual Power Button ❶.

▸ **Filter**:
- There is one additional *State Variable* ❷.
- There is an additional *Spread* parameter ❸.
- The *Envelope* and *LFO* parameters ❹ are just the two renamed "Cutoff Mod" parameters.

▸ **Distortion**:
- The *Input* and *Output* parameters have been renamed to *Pre Filter* and *Post Filter* ❺.
- A new *Mode* popup menu ❻ lets you choose from three options, separately for the Pre Filter and Post Filter.

▸ **Envelope**
- The Envelope is shown as a graph ❼.
- The ADSR parameters can also be set graphically by dragging the Control Points.
- The brightness of a little LED ❽ indicates the envelope stages.

▸ **LFO**:
- A few parameters have been removed: *Decay/Delay, Rate Mod*, and the *Retrigger Button* ❾.
- The brightness of a little LED ❿ indicates the modulation.

10.2

10.2.1

Binaural Post-Processing

The Binaural Post-Processing Plugin only had the Controls View ❶ available, and now it is available with the Editor View ❷.

A few things to pay attention to:

▶ The Plugin will only be listed in the Imaging submenu if the Channel is in stereo mode.

▶ The entire Imaging submenu will not be listed at all in the Plugin Menu if the Channel is set to Surround Mode.

▶ The Parameter *CTC-Speaker Angle* ❸ is only active if the Compensation Mode *"Speaker CTC - Cross Talk Cancellation"* ❹ is selected.

Metering	
BPM Counter	▶
Correlation Meter	▶
Level Meter	▶
MultiMeter	▶
Tuner	▶

Correlation Meter

Two things to note about the Correlation Plugin:

▶ **Horizontal/Vertical View**: Instead of the Editor item, the View Menu displays the item *Horizontal* ❶ and *Vertical* ❷ to display the Plugin in either orientation.

▶ **Plugin Delay Compensation (PDC)**: The timing of the Meters is now correct, following the Plugin Delay Compensation.

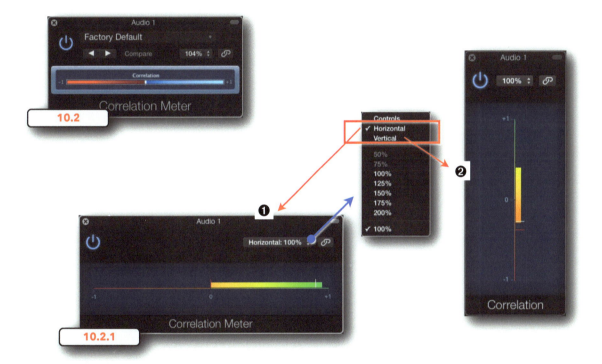

Please note:

The Correlation Meter is only available if the Channel Strip is in stereo. It will not be displayed in mono or surround mode.

Level Meter

There are quite a few changes for the Level Meter Plugin:

- ▶ **Horizontal/Vertical View**: The Plugin can be displayed in Horizontal ❶ or Vertical ❷ orientation.

- ▶ **Surround Mode ❸**: If the Channel Strip is in Surround Mode, then the Level Meter displays all the individual channels. However, it can only display the vertical orientation.

- ▶ **True Peak**: The Level characteristics "Inter Sample Peak" has been renamed to "True Peak" ❹.

- ▶ **RMS Display**: The RMS meter has its separate bars ❺ and its own numeric RMS display ❻.

- ▶ **Target Level**: You can set a "Target Level" between -30dB and 0dB by dragging the yellow insertion line ❼. That's were the meter starts to change from blue to yellow. Numeric Level readouts are also displayed in yellow if they fall in that range.

- ▶ **Target Level Surround**: In surround, the Target Level can be set separately for the LFE, the Center, and the other channels ❽.

- ▶ **Plugin Delay Compensation (PDC)**: The timing of the Meters is now correct, following the Plugin Delay Compensation.

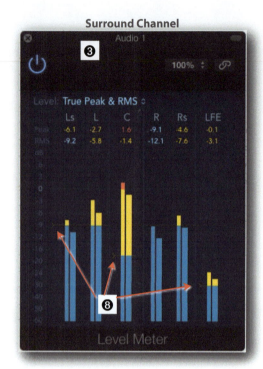

Surround Channel

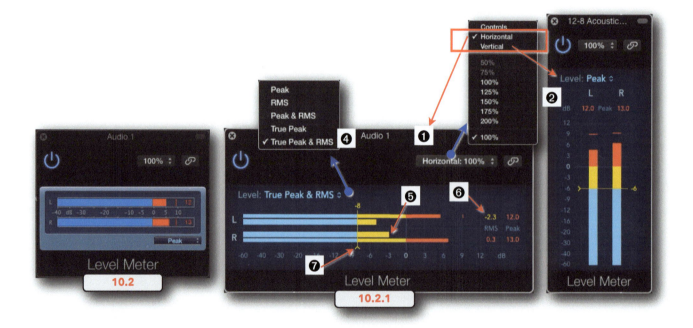

MultiMeter

The MultiMeter also has quite a few changes and improvements:

▶ **Analyzer-Goniometer**: Two big buttons ❶ on top now lets you switch between Analyzer and Goniometer, which switches the layout of the Plugin Window.

▶ **True Peak**: The Level characteristics "Inter Sample Peak" ❷ has been renamed to "True Peak" and can be selected from the *Level* popup menu ❸. Google that important topic to understand the difference between dBFS (dB Full Scale) and dBTP (dB True Peak).

▶ **LUFS**: This is the first time that Logic provides LUFS metering ❹ without requiring a third-party Plugin. This acronym stands for "*Loudness Units relative to Full Scale*", sometimes referred to as "*Loudness K-weighted relative to Full Scale*" (LKFS). Here is a quick read about that topic, but Google around for more info about that important topic. http://www.tcelectronic.com/loudness/loudness-explained/

- LU-I: This number shows the "integrated" Loudness Unit, the loudness over time.
- LU-S: This number shows the "short-term" Loudness Unit, the current reading.

▶ **RMS Display**: The RMS meter now has its separate bars ❺ and its own numeric RMS display.

▶ **Target Level**: You can set a "Target Level" between -30dB and 0dB by dragging the yellow insertion line ❻. The numerical value of the levels will turn yellow ❼ if it falls in that range (between blue and red). You can set the Target Level separate for the LUFS and the Peak/RMS.

▶ **Return Rate [dB/s]**: This new parameter affects the Peak Meter and the Analyzer when set to Peak and determines how fast the meters respond ❽.

▶ **Analyzer Bands**: You can now choose between 31 and 63 Frequency Bands ❾ to be displayed in the Analyzer.

▶ **Plugin Delay Compensation (PDC)**: The timing of the Meters is now correct, following the Plugin Delay Compensation.

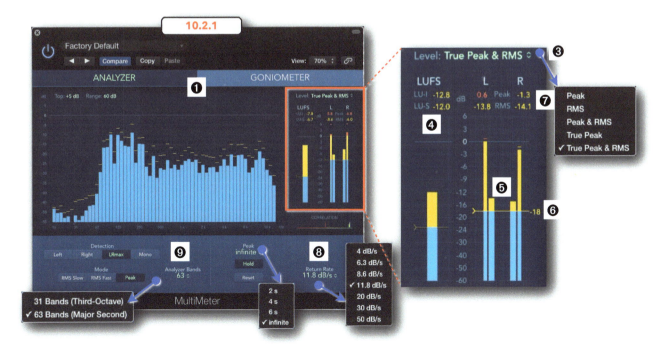

Goniometer

The Goniometer has the same two parameters, *Auto Gain* and *Decay*.

The other parameters and controls are the same for Analyzer and Goniometer.

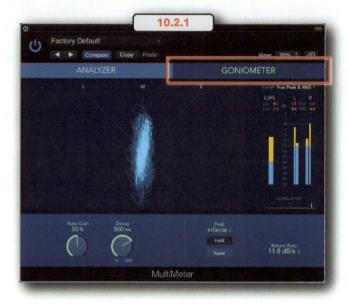

Surround

The surround version of the MultiMeter hasn't been updated yet.

5 - Plugin Makeover

Modulation

Chorus

No changes in the Chorus Plugin besides the face lift.

Ensemble

The Ensemble Plugin has some graphical enhancements:

▸ **Three Waveforms**: Each of the three modulation (LFO1, LFO2, Random) is displayed with its own waveform ❶. Changing the *Rate* and *Intensity* visualizes those parameter changes accordingly.

▸ **Edit Graphically**: You can change the *Rate* and *Intensity* of a modulation graphically by dragging the bulls eye ❷ two-dimensionally. Move the Pointer Tool into that area to make its control visible.

▸ **Modulation on/off**: Each modulation now can be switched on/off independently with the small Power Button ❸.

▸ **Voice Display**: Changing the Voices Control ❹ is reflected in the graphics as a 3D effect ❺ along the waveform.

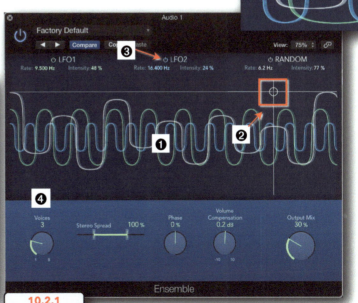

Flanger

There are some additions to the Flanger Plugin:

▶ **LFO Sync**: The *Rate* has a button with a note symbol ❶. This switches the Rate Sync:

  • Rate Sync off (default) ❷: You can set the modulation by frequency from 0Hz to 20kHz.

  • Rate Sync on ❸: You can sync the modulation rate to the tempo of your Project from 32bars to 1/64t.

▶ **Surround Distribution**: If your Channel Strip is set to Surround, then the *Distribution* Parameter will appear, which lets you choose from different Phase Modes ❹.

Microphaser

There are only minor changes to the Microphaser Plugin:

▶ **Editor View**: The Microphaser is one of the Plugins that had only a Controls View ❺. Now, it also has also the blue Editor View.

▶ **LFO Sync**: Like the Flanger, the Microphaser Plugin has the added Sync Button ❻.

Phaser

The new look of the Phaser Plugin has the following improvements:

- ▶ **Reorganized**: The layout of the Parameters are better organized.
- ▶ **LFO Sync**: The two Rate Parameters also have a "LFO1 Sync" 🎵 and "LFO2 Sync" 🎵 button ❶.
- ▶ **Sweep Mode**: The additional "Sweep Mode" ❷ Parameters lets you choose between Squared and Exponential.
- ▶ **Low/Hi Cut Power on/off**: A Power Button lets you turn on/off the High Cut and Low Cut Filter ❸.

Spreader

The Spreader has the same functionality, just a new layout.

Tremolo

The Tremolo has a few minor changes:

▸ **Control Points**: The three parameters *Offset* ❶, *Symmetry* ❷, and *Phase* ❸ are located directly on the Graph. They can be changed by editing the numeric value or dragging the corresponding Control Points ❹ on the graph.

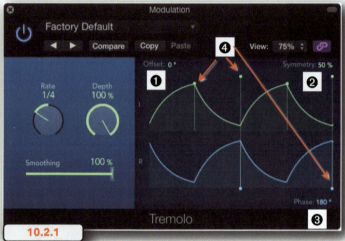

Reverb

EnVerb

The EnVerb Plugin has the same controls with one nice addition:

▶ **Control Points**: You can edit the envelope parameter directly by moving the Control Points ❶ on the graph.

SilverVerb

The SilverVerb has the same functionality, just with a better organized layout, plus one additional control

▶ **Modulation on/off**: A Power Button ❷ lets you turn the Modulation on/off.

Utility (Audio FX Plugin)

Gain

Although the functionality of the Gain Plugin is the same, keep the following in mind:

▸ The available parameters on the Plugin are different when the Channel Strip is in mono ❶, stereo ❷, or surround ❸.

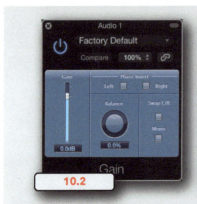

Test Oscillator

There are two changes in the Test Oscillator Plugin:

▸ **Two Views**: You switch between Test Tone Mode ❹ and Sine Sweep Mode ❺ by selecting the big buttons on top. This also changes the view with the available controls.

▸ **Dim Button ❻**: The DIM Button is the only new control. It lowers the output by -18dB when activated.

Please Note:

The Test Oscillator Plugin is also available in the Instrument Plugin Menu under the Utilities menu.

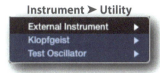

Utility (Instrument Plugin)

Klopfgeist

No changes in the Klopfgeist Plugin besides the new layout and one addition:
   ▶ **Signal LED**: A green LED ❶ indicates the click visually.

*** Compatibility Issues ***

Although, the Plugins are upwards compatible, you can load Logic Projects saved from earlier versions, there are downward compatibility issues due to some of the new or change parameters. If you load a pre-10.2.1 Logic Project, you will get a Dialog Window, giving you the option to do a Save As… of that Project.

6 - Key Commands Changes

Changes

There are some new Key Commands in LPX 10.2.1, some Key Commands have been deleted, and a few got renamed.

New

🌐 Global

▶ Set Division Value to 1/128 Triplet (1/192)
▶ Hide Logic Pro X
▶ Hide Others
▶ Cycle through window views
▶ Cycle through window views (counter-clockwise)
▶ Minimize All Windows

🌐 Mixer

▶ Create Track Stack for Selected Channel Strips
▶ Flatten Track Stack for Selected Channel Strips

🌐 EXS Instrument Editor

▶ New Instrument
▶ Open Instrument
▶ Save Instrument As...
▶ Rename Instrument…
▶ Open in Audio File Editor
▶ Select Zone of Last Played Key

🌐 Main Window Tracks

▶ Hide All Empty Tracks

🌐 Main Window Tracks and Various Editors

▶ Snap Mode: As Time Quantization
▶ Select Next Event of Same Type
▶ Select Previous Event of Same Type
▶ Open Chord Grid Library…

Deleted

Global

▶ Adjust Tempo using Beat Detection

Global Control Surfaces Commands

▶ Scan All Models
▶ Main Window Tracks
▶ Write Automation to End
▶ Write Automation to Right Locator

Renamed

Global

▶ Move Movie Region to Project Start ➤ Move Movie Region (and SMPTE Position) to Project Start
▶ Move Movie Region to Playhead ➤ Move Movie Region (and SMPTE Position) to Playhead

Score

▶ Next Event ➤ Select Next Event
▶ Previous Event ➤ Select Previous Event

This concludes my manual " *Logic Pro X - What's New in 10.2.1".*

If you find my visual approach of explaining features and concepts helpful, please recommend my books to others or maybe write a review on Amazon or the iBooks Store. This will help me to continue this series.
To check out other books in my "Graphically Enhanced Manuals" series, go to my website at:

www.DingDingMusic.com/Manuals

To contact me directly, email me at: GEM@DingDingMusic.com

More information about my day job as a composer and links to my social network sites are on my website:
www.DingDingMusic.com

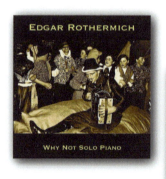

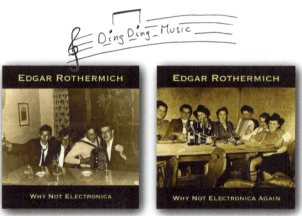

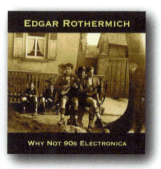

Listen to my music on SoundCloud

Thanks for your interest and your support,

Edgar Rothermich